QUEBEC

PROVINCE DIVIDED

QUEBEC

PROVINCE DIVIDED

by Peter Kizilos

Lerner Publications Company / Minneapolis

Lerner Publications Company
A Division of Lerner Publishing Group
241 First Avenue North
Minneapolis, MN 55401 U.S.A.

Website address: www.lernerbooks.com

All maps by Philip Schwartzberg, Meridian Mapping, Minneapolis.
Cover photo by CP Picture Archive/Moe Doiron
Table of contents photos (from top to bottom) by Reuters/Peter Jones/Archive Photos;
National Archives of Canada/C393; AP/World Wide Photos; Phil Norton

Series Consultant: Andrew Bell-Fialkoff
Editor: Kari Cornell
Editorial Director: Mary M. Rodgers
Designer: Michael Tacheny
Photo Researcher: Glenn Marier

LIBRARY OF CONGRESS CATALOGING-IN-PUBLICATION DATA

Kizilos, Peter.
    Quebec : province divided / by Peter Kizilos.
        p. cm. — (World in Conflict)
    Includes bibliographical references and index.
    Summary: Examines the history of the Canadian province's ethnic conflict as French
    speakers have struggled to preserve their cultural, religious, and ethnic identity in an English-
    speaking country and how that struggle has led to the movement to make Quebec
    an independent country.
    ISBN 0–8225–3562–9 (lib. bdg. : alk. paper)
1. Quebec (Province)—History—Autonomy and independence movements Juvenile literature.
2. Quebec (Province)—Politics and government—1960– Juvenile literature. 3. Canada—Politics
and government—1980– Juvenile literature. 4. Canada—Ethnic relations Juvenile literature.
[1. Quebec (Province)—History—Autonomy and independence movements. 2. Quebec
(Province)—Politics and government—1960– 3. Canada—Politics and government—1980–
Canada—Ethnic relations.] I. Title. II. Series.

F1053.2.K59   2000
971.4'04-dc21   99-17667

Manufactured in the United States of America
1 2 3 4 5 6 – JR – 05 04 03 02 01 00

CONTENTS

ABOUT THIS SERIES

Government firepower kills 25 protesters . . . . Thousands of refugees flee the country . . . . Rebels attack capital . . . . Racism and rage flare . . . . Fighting breaks out . . . . Peace talks stall . . . . Bombing toll rises to 52 . . . . Slaughter has cost up to 50,000 lives.

Conflicts between people occur across the globe, and we hear about some of the more spectacular and horrific episodes in the news. But since most fighting doesn't directly affect us, we often choose to ignore it. And even if we do take the time to learn about these conflicts—from newspapers, magazines, television news, or radio—we're often left with just a snapshot of the conflict instead of the whole reel of film.

Most news accounts don't tell you the whole story about a conflict, focusing instead on the attention-grabbing events that make the headlines. In addition, news sources may have a preconceived idea about who is right and who is wrong in a conflict. The stories that result often portray one side as the "bad guys" and the other as the "good guys."

The *World in Conflict* series approaches each conflict with the idea that wars and political disputes aren't simply about bullies and victims. Conflicts are complex problems that can often be traced back hundreds of years. The people fighting one another have complicated reasons for doing so. Fighting erupts between groups divided by ethnicity, religion, and nationalism. These groups fight over power, money, territory, control. Sometimes people who just want to go about their own business get caught up in a conflict just because they're there.

These books examine major conflicts around the world, some of which are very bloody and others that haven't involved a lot of violence. They portray the people involved in and affected by conflicts. They describe how each conflict got started, how it developed, and where it stands. The books also outline some of the ways people have tried to end the conflicts. By reading the stories behind the headlines, you will learn some reasons why people hate and fight one another and, in addition, why some people struggle so hard to end conflicts.

WORDS YOU NEED TO KNOW

assimilate: To absorb into the culture of a population or group by adopting their language, customs, and beliefs.

British Commonwealth: An organization of self-governing autonomous states that share a common allegiance to the British crown.

confederation: The alliance of states or nations for mutual support or common action.

conscription: The forced enrollment of persons for military service.

dominion: A self-governing nation of the British Commonwealth other than the United Kingdom that acknowledges the British monarch as chief of state.

federalist: One who favors a strong central government and much weaker provincial governments.

hard-liner: One who believes so strongly in a certain philosophy that he or she refuses to compromise. In Quebec, for example, PQ hard-liners see no alternative to secession.

Loyalists: A group of British colonists who migrated north to Quebec during the American Revolution in order to continue living under British rule.

nation: A community of people from one or more ethnic groups that lives in a defined territory and has its own government. By this definition, a nation is not necessarily the same as a country. Within Canada, "nation" has two different meanings. Federalists are likely to define Canada as a nation while most sovereigntists will call the province of Quebec a nation.

popular vote: In a parliamentary system, the votes cast by registered voters for a local political candidate, who stands for a particular political party. Under this system, the voters choose only their local representative. Political power—that is, who will be prime minister—goes to the person who heads whichever party won the most seats. As such, a local candidate could win the popular vote in a district, but the candidate's party may not gain the premiership.

provincialism: Relating to or coming from a province.

secede: To formally withdraw membership from a political unit, such as a nation, or from an organization, such as the United Nations. The seceding group usually desires increased independence or autonomy.

secular: Of or relating to the state instead of to the church.

seigneurial: A system of land distribution in which the king granted a portion of land to a company. The company, in turn, distributed it in lots to influential people (called seigneurs) who then leased the lots to farmers.

sovereigntist: One who favors a decentralized system in which the provincial government holds the most authority. Many sovereigntists in Quebec want the province to secede from Canada and become its own country.

sovereignty: Power over a region. In some cases, an outside political entity holds the power; in others, a region has its own independent political control.

FOREWORD

by Andrew Bell-Fialkoff

Conflicts between various groups are as old as time. Peoples and tribes around the world have fought one another for thousands of years. In fact our history is in great part a succession of wars—between the Greeks and the Persians, the English and the French, the Russians and the Poles, and many others. Not only do states or ethnic groups fight one another, so do followers of different religions—Catholics and Protestants in Northern Ireland, Christians and Muslims in Bosnia, and Buddhists and Hindus in Sri Lanka. Often ethnicity, language, and religion—some of the main distinguishing elements of culture—reinforce one another in characterizing a particular group. For instance, the vast majority of Greeks are Orthodox Christian and speak Greek; most Italians are Roman Catholic and speak Italian. Elsewhere, one cultural aspect predominates. Serbs and Croats speak dialects of the same language but remain separate from one another because most Croats are Catholics and most Serbs are Orthodox Christians. To those two groups, religion is more important than language in defining culture.

We have witnessed an increasing number of conflicts in modern times—why? Three reasons stand out. One is that large empires—such as Austria-Hungary, Ottoman Turkey, several colonial empires with vast holdings in Asia, Africa, and America, and, most recently, the Soviet Union—have collapsed. A look at world maps from 1900, 1950, and 1998 reveals an ever-increasing number of small and medium-sized states. While empires existed, their rulers suppressed many ethnic and religious conflicts. Empires imposed order, and local resentments were mostly directed at the central authority. Inside the borders of empires, populations were multiethnic and often highly mixed. When the empires fell apart, world leaders found it impossible to establish political frontiers that coincided with ethnic boundaries. Different groups often claimed territories inhabited by others. The nations created on the lands of a toppled empire were saddled with acute border and ethnic problems from their very beginnings.

The second reason for more conflicts in modern times stems from the twin ideals of freedom and equality. In the United States, we usually think of freedom as "individual freedom." If we all have equal rights, we are free. But if you are a member of a minority group and feel that you are being discriminated against, your group's rights and freedoms are also important to you. In fact, if you don't have your "group freedom," you don't have full individual freedom either.

After World War I (1914–1918), the allied western nations, under the guidance of U.S. president Woodrow Wilson, tried to satisfy group rights by promoting minority rights. The spread of frantic nationalism in the 1930s, especially among disaffected ethnic minorities, and the catastrophe of World War II (1939–1945) led to a fundamental reassessment of the Wilsonian philosophy. After 1945 group rights were downplayed on the assumption that guaranteeing individual rights would be sufficient. In later decades, the collapse of multiethnic nations like Czechoslovakia, Yugoslavia, and the Soviet Union—coupled with the spread of nationalism in those regions—came as a shock to world leaders. People want democracy and individual rights, but they want their group rights, too. In practice, this means more conflicts and a cycle of secession, as minority ethnic groups seek their own sovereignty and independence.

The fires of conflict are often further stoked by the media, which lavishes glory and attention on independence movements. To fight for freedom is an honor. For every Palestinian who has killed an Israeli, there are hundreds of Kashmiris, Tamils, and Bosnians eager to shoot at their enemies. Newspapers, television and radio news broadcasts, and other media play a vital part in fomenting that sense of honor. They magnify each crisis, glorify rebellion, and help to feed the fire of conflict.

The third factor behind increasing conflict in the world is the social and geographic mobility that modern society enjoys. We can move anywhere we want and can aspire—or so we believe—to be anything we wish. Every day the television tantalizingly dangles the prizes that life can offer. We all want our share. But increased mobility and ambition also mean increased competition, which leads to antagonism. Antagonism often fastens itself to ethnic, racial, or religious differences. If you are an inner-city African American and your local grocer happens to be Korean American, you may see that individual as different from yourself—an intruder—rather than as a person, a neighbor, or a grocer. This same feeling of "us" versus "them" has been part of many an ethnic conflict around the world.

Many conflicts have been contained—even solved—by wise, responsible leadership. But unfortunately, many politicians use citizens' discontent for their own ends. They incite hatred, manipulate voters, and mobilize people against their neighbors. The worst things happen when neighbor turns against neighbor. In Bosnia, in Rwanda, in Lebanon, and in countless other places, people who had lived and worked together and had even intermarried went on a rampage, killing, raping, and robbing one another with gusto. If the appalling carnage teaches us anything, it is that we should stop seeing one another as hostile competitors and enemies and accept one another as people. Most importantly, we should learn to understand why conflicts happen and how they can be prevented. That is why *World in Conflict* is so important—the books in this series will help you understand the history and inner dynamics of some of the most persistent conflicts of modern times. And understanding is the first step to prevention. ⊕

INTRODUCTION

Je me souviens ("I remember" in French) is the motto on the license plate of every car and truck in the Canadian province of Quebec. The slogan, stamped in royal blue, recalls the days of French rule in Quebec, the era before 1759. After that date, Britain took over. The slogan is a highly visible reminder of Quebec's past and of the conflict that continues to divide its people.

THE CONFLICT

It's been a long time, but French-speaking Quebecers haven't forgotten the resentment their ancestors felt about the British takeover. As part of English-speaking Canada, the province of Quebec remains an island of French culture and language. Throughout the province's history, French speakers, called Francophones, have struggled to preserve their distinct cultural, religious, and ethnic identity in an English-speaking country that has often tried to **assimilate** them. Francophones have fought to preserve their culture by enforcing language preservation laws in Quebec and by maintaining a French social system.

But many Francophones believe that their identity is endangered as long as they remain a minority within the rest of English-speaking Canada. Some believe that the only way to preserve and protect their identity is for Quebec to leave Canada and to become a separate and independent country with its own foreign policy and armed forces.

In 1980 and again in 1995, Quebecers had the opportunity to vote on Quebec's **sovereignty.** In both referendums (public votes), the people of Quebec chose to remain a province of Canada. But in each election, the number of people voting to **secede** increased. Since 1995 leaders of Quebec pro-independence organizations have pledged to hold another referendum.

Covering nearly 600,000 square miles, Quebec is Canada's largest province.

Baffin Island

Hudson Strait

Ungava
Bay

Hudson Bay

Labrador
Sea

Newfoundland and Labrador

James
Bay

*Canadian
Shield*

Quebec

St. Lawrence River

Gaspé
Peninsula

Gulf of
St. Lawrence

C A N A D A

New
Brunswick

Prince
Edward
Island

St. Maurice R.

Quebec
City ◉

● Charlottetown

Ottawa R.

Trois-Rivières ●

Montreal ●

Ottawa ○

Ontario

UNITED
STATES

*Nova
Scotia*

*ATLANTIC
OCEAN*

Lake Ontario

○ Ottawa	National Capital
◉ Quebec City	Provincial Capital
● Montreal	Major City
CANADA	Country Name
Quebec	Province Name
–··–··–	International Border
–·–·–·–	Provincial Border

over 1,800 feet
1,200 feet
600 feet
sea level

0   100   200 miles

0   100   200   300 kilometers

Over the years, the focus of the sovereignty movement in Quebec has shifted from preservation of French-Canadian culture to the desire to rally all Quebecers to assert control over issues and resources of the province. The **sovereigntists'** desire to protect and assert their identity as a **nation** has created tension both within Quebec and between Quebec and Canada's other provinces. English speakers in Quebec, called Anglophones, have protested that provincial laws designed to protect the French language restrict their right to speak freely and to participate fully in the life of their province. They claim the language laws also limit their access to government services, jobs, and schools. Anglophones are living in a primarily English-speaking country and expect that their rights as Canadian citizens should be respected. Because of these problems, many Anglophones have chosen to leave a province where they no longer feel welcome.

THE LAND

In terms of sheer size, Canada is the second largest country in the world, com-

Put Yourself in Their Shoes

French speakers living in any Canadian province besides Quebec or New Brunswick—the two provinces that offer the most services to their minority groups—have far fewer rights than do English speakers living in Quebec. Except for coping with the enforcement of the province's language laws, Anglophones enjoy a relatively high quality of life.

Under the 1867 constitution, Quebecers are guaranteed bilingualism in all legislative and judicial matters—a right that does not exist in other provinces. Under Quebec law, educational and health services located in English-speaking communities must be offered in English. Quebec has 340 English-language elementary and secondary schools, 7 English-language colleges, and 3 English-language universities. The Quebec government, which controls the province's education system, mandates that both public and private English schools are eligible for public funding. And, finally, English speakers in Quebec have access to a wide range of English television stations, radio stations, newspapers, magazines, and other media produced in English.

French speakers living in other provinces (again, with the exception of New Brunswick) are not so lucky. Even though the federal government has established Canada as a bilingual country, each province chooses to enforce language laws differently.

prising a total land area of more than 3.8 million square miles. Quebec is the largest of Canada's 10 provinces and 3 territories. With an area of about 594,862 square miles, Quebec is roughly three times the size of France.

Located in eastern Canada, Quebec shares its border with three Canadian provinces and with four states of the United

States. The province of Ontario touches Quebec's western side and wraps around the province's southwestern corner. Newfoundland and Labrador borders Quebec in the east, and the province of New Brunswick touches Quebec's southeastern edge. To the south, Quebec and the United States meet at the borders of

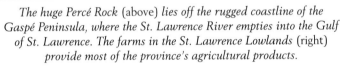

The huge Percé Rock (above) *lies off the rugged coastline of the Gaspé Peninsula, where the St. Lawrence River empties into the Gulf of St. Lawrence. The farms in the St. Lawrence Lowlands* (right) *provide most of the province's agricultural products.*

Maine, New Hampshire, Vermont, and New York.

Water flanks northern Quebec on all sides. The Hudson Bay washes most of the province's western border, while the Hudson Strait separates Quebec from Baffin Island to the north. The most important waterway in Quebec, the St. Lawrence River, cuts through the southeastern part of the province. The river, which begins in Lake Ontario and flows north-eastward until it empties into the Gulf of St. Lawrence, provides an important link between Great Lakes cities—such as Duluth, Chicago, Detroit, and Toronto—and the Atlantic Ocean.

Quebec's terrain can be divided into three main areas—the Canadian Shield, the St. Lawrence Lowlands, and the Appalachian Region. The Canadian Shield, an elevated region mostly within northern Quebec, makes up about 90 percent of the province's total land area. Formed by glaciers during the Ice Age, the Canadian Shield also covers about half of Canada. This flat region is rocky, forested, and dotted with lakes. Abundant minerals, such as nickel and copper, lie beneath the shield's surface.

To the south, a fertile agricultural region called the St. Lawrence Lowlands borders the St. Lawrence River. About 90 percent of Quebec's total population lives in this region, which includes the major cities of Montreal and Quebec City, the Eastern Townships, and the Ottawa Valley. Montreal, the province's bustling commercial hub, is a large and culturally diverse metropolis. Quebec City is the provincial capital and the cradle of Quebec's French culture. The Eastern Townships and the Ottawa Valley comprise the land along Quebec's border with the United States. Commercial farmers in the lowlands grow grain, tobacco, fruit, and vegetables. Quebec is the leading producer of butter and cheese in Canada, and most of the province's dairy farms are also located in this fertile region.

South of the St. Lawrence Lowlands is the Appalachian Region. This area is an extension of the Appalachian Mountain chain that begins in the southern United States and stretches through southeastern Quebec to the tip of the Gaspé Peninsula.

THE ECONOMY

Relatively prosperous and productive, Quebec provides its citizens with a high standard of living compared to the rest of the world. The province has an abundance of natural resources, especially minerals and water. Quebec's northern region yields rich reserves of copper, iron, zinc, silver, and gold. Plentiful forests supply pulp for strong paper and lumber industries.

Although Quebec has almost no coal, oil, or natural

©Tourisme Québec/Sylvain Majeau

The Château Frontenac, a castlelike hotel, rises dramatically above Quebec City, the oldest city in Canada. Quebec City is the heart of Francophone culture and the home of the only Francophone government in North America.

gas deposits, it has developed a strong manufacturing industry by tapping its huge hydroelectric power potential. Hydro-Québec, a public corporation controlled by Quebec's provincial government, is Canada's largest producer of electricity. Hydro-Québéc's 50 separate power plants, located throughout the province, produce 80 percent of Quebec's electric power and nearly half of the nation's total hydroelectric power.

One of Quebec's most important resources is the St. Lawrence River, located in the southeastern part of the province. Since 1959—when engineers created the St. Lawrence Seaway by widening the portion of the river that stretches between Montreal and Lake Ontario—the St. Lawrence River has become a frequently used international shipping channel. The building of the seaway gave a major boost to U.S.–Canadian trade. Any change in Quebec's sovereignty could affect the flow of goods from Quebec and other parts of Canada through the St. Lawrence Seaway. This, in turn, could have major implications for

© James P. Rowan

The St. Lawrence River, an international shipping route, plays an important role in the economies of Quebec and Canada. Cargo ships transport Canadian products to ports all over the world.

Canada's trade with the United States, its largest trading partner, and with other global trading partners.

GOVERNMENT

Canada is a federation of provinces and territories. Under a federalist system, certain powers are reserved for the national government, while the remaining powers are in the hands of the provinces. In Canada provincial governments are granted a great deal of autonomy over their own affairs. A

cabinet, led by a prime minister, controls the federal government. The Constitution Act of 1982 declares that Great Britain's monarch, who is represented in Canada by a governor-general, is the head of state. Over the years, however, British representation has become merely symbolic. A two-house parliament passes laws on issues within the realm of the federal government. Members of Parliament's House of Commons are elected, while its senate members are appointed. Population determines the number of house seats granted to each province. As a general rule, the leader of the party that wins the greatest number of Parliment seats becomes prime minister. The prime minister chooses cabinet members from his or her party. The governor-general makes the senate appointments, under the prime minister's guidance.

At the provincial level, the 125-member National Assembly rules Quebec. Voters elect all members. The leader of the party that wins the most assembly seats becomes the premier of Quebec. The premier selects ministers for the Executive Council—the organization that sets policy, applies laws, and runs the province—from among the party's elected members. Elected National Assembly members of the party that placed second make up the official opposition—which keeps the majority-led government in check.

THE PEOPLE OF QUEBEC

The legacy left by Quebec's French and English settlers in the sixteenth, seventeenth,

Canadian Federalism

Canada's national and provincial governments are based on a system called federalism. Powers are divided among a central, or federal, government and many provincial governments. The federal government maintains jurisdiction over the entire country, while provincial governments oversee local matters. A written constitution dictates which powers reside with the federal government and which powers provincial governments handle.

A federalist government may be centralized or decentralized. In a centralized federalist government—such as that of the United States—the majority of power is in the hands of the national government, and states or provinces hold less authority. Canada, on the other hand, is an example of a decentralized federalist system, in which provinces wield more control. Under this kind of system, provinces function as nation-states within the larger country.

Throughout Canada's history, the federalist system has fluctuated between centralization and decentralization, depending upon political, economic, and social variables. After 1960, however, Quebec leader Jean Lesage pushed the federal government to decentralize and grant more authority to the provinces. At that time, other provinces had little interest in taking on more control. So the federal government proposed the concept of special status,

and eighteenth centuries is a distinct society set apart from the rest of Canada. The most profound difference between Quebecers and Canadians in the rest of the country is language. While Canada has two official languages, English and French, the majority of Canadians speak English. French is the official language of Quebec, and it is spoken by 90 percent of the province's inhabitants.

Language remains a major defining factor within Quebec, too. Although Quebec's ethnicity is intricate and varied, its population can be divided into four main groups. People of French ancestry make up the largest ethnic group. Many Francophones are Québécois—Quebecers who whereby Quebec would become the sole province with additional powers.

Debates continue over how to establish such status and about whether Quebec should be granted such privileges at all. The conflict boils down to a clash between the two concepts of federalism. Federalists believe that the federal government should be the main government. As the senior power, the federal government has the capacity to establish national standards by which all provincial laws must abide. In this same vein, the federal government can choose to maintain total control over certain legislation. Most English-speaking Canadians, who see the federal government as their national government serving all of Canada, share this view. In general federalists see any decentralization of powers as weakening Canada.

Many Francophones see federalism in a different light. To them, the Quebec government is best able to represent their main interests. Therefore the provincial government should have the most power. This group holds that Québécois should make up their own nation and that such a nation ought to govern the majority of its affairs. Québécois argue that if the federal government continues to refuse to acknowledge the multinational nature of Canadian society and the right of each province to govern itself, Quebec must seek sovereignty.

trace their ancestry back to the first 12,000 or so French men and women who settled the area in the late seventeenth century. A large percentage of the Francophone population is Roman Catholic. Francophones tend to be very proud of their heritage and many identify themselves as Québécois first and as Canadians second. Most Francophones live in Quebec City or in Montreal. Others dwell in more rural areas scattered throughout the St. Lawrence Lowlands. About one-third of Francophones are bilingual, speaking both French and English.

Anglophones are a second large group, representing roughly 10 percent of Quebec's total population. Many Anglophones are descended from British **Loyalists** who fled Britain's American colonies on the eve of the Revolutionary War in 1776. The vast majority of Anglophones and **federalists** live in and around Quebec's larger cities, especially Montreal. Most Anglophones are Protestants, and they tend to identify themselves as Canadians or English Canadians first and as Quebecers second.

The indigenous peoples of the province, who lived in Quebec long before the arrival of any Europeans, make up a third important segment of Quebec society. This group includes the Inuit and North American Indians such as the Cree, the Huron, and the Mohawk. These Quebecers speak a variety of languages, including Inuktitut and Cree. According to the 1991 census, there were about 50,000 Inuits and about 80,000 North American Indians living in Quebec.

The Cree and the Inuit live along the coasts of Hudson Bay and Ungava Bay in the resource-rich north. This area includes James Bay, part of Hudson Bay and the site of Quebec's largest

This Inuit woman and her child are part of Quebec's large native population, which lives in the northern two-thirds of the province. Native Canadians have demanded a say in the province's political future.

immigrants who have come to Quebec since World War II (1939–1945). Most of these new immigrants, from countries such as Italy, Greece, China, Portugal, and Poland, speak a first language other than French or English. In Quebec they are called Allophones. Because of Quebec's liberal immigration policies, the Allophone population has grown rapidly to about 800,000, or roughly equal to the size of the Anglophone population. Allophones have helped create rich ethnic and cultural diversity in Quebec, especially in Montreal.

In recent years, Quebec has also specifically encouraged French-speaking immigrants to settle in the province from such distant places as

Haiti (in the Caribbean) and the African nation of Morocco. Although these new Quebecers speak French, the vast majority want their children to learn English so that they can get ahead in Canadian society.

TAKING SIDES

The ongoing clash between Francophones and Anglophones is most evident in disputes over language rights, access to education and to government services, and in debates over Quebec's relationship with the rest of Canada. The two major groups involved in the conflict over Quebec's independence are the sovereigntists and the federalists.

The political parties that favor remaining within

hydroelectric power plant. Groups like the Huron and the Mohawk live on reserves, many of which are clustered along the St. Lawrence River in southeastern Quebec. Some reserves have the power to regulate their own affairs within the territory under their control.

A fourth major group of Quebecers consists of new

Anglophones in Quebec

Quebec's Anglophone population has significantly declined in the past 20 years. Many young Anglophones have chosen to leave Quebec, often citing the difficulty of living and working in a province where they are a linguistic minority. At the same time, the Anglophones who have chosen to stay in Quebec are more likely to learn French than ever before. In the past two decades, the percentage of bilingual Anglophones has increased from 32 percent to about 62 percent. Some Anglophones are even speaking French at home, marking the first time in Quebec's history that English speakers are assimilating into French culture.

Canada are referred to as federalists. The Liberal Party and the English-rights Equality Party are the largest federalist parties. Most Anglophones, Allophones, and indigenous Canadians support the federalists.

Most supporters of the sovereigntist cause are Francophones. Representing the sovereigntists are two major political parties—the Parti Québécois (PQ) at the provincial level (dubbed *pequistes* by the French-language media) and the Bloc Québécois (BQ) at the

Many want Quebec to remain in Canada because the province's strong French flavor is one of the main things that distinguishes Canadian culture and society from those of the United States.

national level. Both parties were strong supporters of a 1995 referendum on Quebec sovereignty.

The divisions in this province are neither clear nor simple, however. Not all Francophones are sovereigntists. In the 1995 referendum on Quebec independence,

60 percent of eligible Francophone voters voted for independence, but 40 percent voted against it.

People througout the rest of Canada are also concerned about the sovereigntist movement. Many want Quebec to remain in Canada because the province's strong French flavor is one of the main things that distinguishes Canadian culture and society from those of the United States. Many Canadians also believe that Quebec makes an important contribution to Canada's economy, political strength, and stability. Other Canadians are concerned about setting a bad precedent. If Quebec were to be allowed to leave Canada, what would stop the country's other provinces from breaking away? Some Canadians fear that allowing Quebec to part ways with Canada could lead to the weakening or dissolution of Canada as a country. ⊕

© Dick Hemingway

Je me souviens serves as a daily reminder of Quebec's French heritage.

MAJOR PLAYERS IN THE CONFLICT

Lucien Bouchard

Jean Chrétien

Stephen Dion

Bertrand, Guy A lawyer from Quebec City and a former member of the Parti Québécois, Bertrand has become a strong proponent of federalism in recent years.

Bloc Québécois (BQ) Founded by Lucien Bouchard and other Quebec sovereigntists after the Meech Lake Accord failed in 1990, the BQ is a national political party that favors Quebec sovereignty. Members of the BQ serve in the Canadian Parliament.

Bouchard, Lucien Leader of the BQ until 1995, when he left to become Quebec's premier after Premier Jacques Parizeau resigned. A strong leader of the sovereigntist movement, Bouchard has been resistant to compromise during negotiations with the federalist national government.

Charest, Jean Leader of the Quebec Liberal Party since the spring of 1998, Charest came close to edging out Lucien Bouchard in the November 1998 election.

Chrétien, Jean Elected prime minister of Canada in 1993, Jean Chrétien is a member of the Liberal Party and a federalist. Chrétien has sought to negotiate a peaceful resolution to the conflict between Quebec and the rest of Canada. Although he has been willing to support some efforts to recognize Quebec's status as a distinct society, he has firmly rejected any proposal that would lead to separation from Canada.

Dion, Stephen Appointed by Prime Minister Jean Chrétien as the minister of intergovernmental affairs in November 1995, Stephen Dion leads the national government's efforts to peacefully resolve the conflict between Quebec and the rest of Canada.

Liberal Party

Liberal Party Formed in the late 1800s, the Liberal Party has dominated the Canadian political scene throughout the twentieth century. The Liberal Party is the biggest federalist political party, with branches at both the provincial and national levels.

Parizeau, Jacques Leader of the Parti Québécois.

Parti Québécois (PQ) Founded in the early 1970s, the PQ is the provincial political party dedicated to advancing the cause of Quebec sovereignty. Leaders of the PQ, such as René Lévesque, were largely responsible for reviving Francophone interest in Quebec's independence after the defeat of the 1980 referendum on sovereignty-association.

Reuters/Ralph Alswang/Archive Photos

Jacques Parizeau

Parti Québécois

CHAPTER

1

THE RECENT CONFLICT AND ITS EFFECTS

Monday, October 30, 1995, was a far from typical day on the streets of Montreal and Quebec City. On this date, Quebecers were asked for the second time to vote on a referendum deciding the future of their province. Those who voted *Oui* (yes) would be voting in favor of Quebec breaking away from Canada and becoming a separate and independent country. Those who cast *Non* (no) votes wanted Quebec to remain part of Canada.

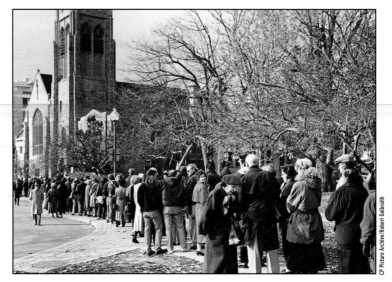

On Monday, October 30, 1995, Quebecers waited in line to vote on the referendum that would decide the fate of their province.

WHAT WOULD IT MEAN?

While it was clear that the referendum would have major consequences for Quebec and for all of Canada, many people wondered what those consequences might be. For example, how would a victory for the Oui side affect Quebec's economy? It was not known whether Quebecers would still use Canadian currency or if they would continue to use Canadian passports. And there was no guarantee that those who voted against sovereignty would retain their rights as Canadian citizens. Some federalists argued that if Quebec's Francophones could decide their own destiny, then regions within the province with large Anglophone and Allophone populations should be allowed to break away from an independent Quebec to remain within the Canadian fold. Federalists also reasoned that an independent Quebec should be expected to pay off its share of Canada's national debt, a request to which sovereigntists agreed.

What if the Non side won? Some thought it might spell the end of Quebec's sovereigntist movement. Others were concerned that it could spark renewed conflict in the province. There was no telling whether Quebec would remain a rebellious and resentful member of the Canadian federation, or if the province would actively seek to bridge the gap between the provincial and national governments. Lingering uncertainty about Quebec's future would most likely affect the province's relationship with the rest of Canada and with other countries.

BEFORE
THE REFERENDUM

While outside observers struggle to make sense of the conflict, the issues are well known to people in Quebec and in the rest of Canada. The split between French-speaking and English-speaking Quebecers has been a fact of life for many years. Francophones have a long list of grievances. They resent lingering economic dispari-

In 1994 Jacques Parizeau became the premier of Quebec. His outspoken support for sovereignty gave new life to the campaign for secession.

Reuters/Ralph Alswang/Archive Photos

ties between French- and English-speaking Quebecers, and they feel as though they've been treated as second-class citizens throughout Canadian history. French-speaking Quebecers also fear that their language and culture will not survive

unless it's given special protection by English-speaking Canada. Francophone worries have been amplified by the Canadian government's repeated failure to address Francophone concerns through constitutional measures.

In September 1994, Francophones made their voices heard. They elected Jacques Parizeau, a leader of the PQ, as premier of Quebec. Their support was based on his promise to hold a referendum on independence shortly after taking office. Parizeau and other sovereigntist leaders in the PQ and the BQ continued to argue that the only way to preserve and to strengthen Quebec's distinct culture and heritage was to declare the province's independence.

In the summer of 1995, however, political polls showed that Quebecers were divided and confused on the issue of Quebec's sovereignty. While 55 percent opposed independence, most did not fully understand the terms of the referendum. Polls showed that many Quebecers were likely to reject a strongly worded referendum that emphasized a Quebec completely independent from Canada. Even among the referendum's opponents, some were planning to vote Oui just to give Quebec more leverage when it went to the table to negotiate a new relationship with the rest of Canada.

To buy time to build support for independence, Parizeau and his supporters delayed the referendum. The PQ also toned down its wording to try to win the maximum number of Oui votes. That is, instead of asking Quebecers to vote on secession, the referendum asked whether voters agreed that Quebec should "become sovereign after having made a formal offer to Canada for a new economic and political partnership." In other words, before making a decision on separation, Quebec would first need to propose a new political and economic relationship with Canada. Only if the proposal was made and then rejected by the rest of Canada would Quebec's provincial government be able to move ahead with plans for separation.

Controversy swirled around the upcoming referendum and its wording. As a result, Parizeau stepped down as head of the Oui campaign, and Lucien Bouchard, leader of the BQ, took over. The more charismatic and popular Bouchard was an effective campaigner who could rouse sovereigntist fervor in support of independence.

With the date of the referendum approaching, Oui and Non supporters mounted vigorous campaigns. Both sides sponsored town hall meetings and public rallies throughout Quebec. With speeches, campaign literature, internet sites, and television, radio, and newspaper advertisements, supporters in both camps worked hard to win votes. Polls showed that Quebecers were evenly divided on the independence issue. The two campaigns roared on until the last possible minute.

Public interest in the impending vote was obvious. Quebec was plastered with Oui and Non banners and posters. Both federalists and sovereigntists used the

Reuters/Peter Jones/Archive Photos

In the weeks leading up to the referendum, Quebecers expressed their opinions on the upcoming vote. While Oui supporters (facing page) *marched for secession, unity rally attendees* (right) *showed support for keeping Quebec in Canada.*

CP Picture Archive/Ryan Remiorz

blue-and-white fleur-de-lis, the provincial symbol of Quebec, to show that their position was the truly patriotic one. A few days before the vote, more than 150,000 Canadians from across the country gathered in Montreal's Place du Montreal to show support for federal unity. Cheering crowds chanted "Non, Non, Non" to separation and waved banners and signs in both English and French that read "We belong together," "My Canada includes Quebec," and *C'est mieux ensemble* ("It's better together"). Sovereigntist supporters accused the unity

rally organizers of sponsoring an event that violated campaign financing laws. Specifically, they charged that organizers had accepted financial support for the event from groups outside Quebec without prior authorization from provincial election officials.

On election eve, thousands of young Francophones crowded into Quebec City's ice hockey arena to wave blue-and-white banners and sing songs denouncing the federalists. Some wore T-shirts that read *Quebec aux Québécois,* which can mean one of two things. "Quebec for all Quebecers"

has been used as a civic slogan to promote the notion that all citizens of Quebec should fully control their own destiny. The French-Canadian majority has also used it as an ethnic slogan to reaffirm itself as a group seeking full power over Quebec.

THE VOTE AND ITS AFTERMATH

As the first ballots trickled in on election night, Canadians across the country waited for the outcome. In the event of a Oui vote, the PQ planned to start independence negotiations between Quebec's National Assembly and the federal government immediately. Quebec's minister of international affairs had already dispatched letters to foreign embassies in Canada, calling on them to recognize the new country. PQ leaders were expecting France to furnish an especially hearty endorsement of support. They hoped French support would spark a similar move by the United States. Parizeau's victory speech was written and ready to go.

Interest in the referendum was high—94 percent of eligible voters participated. In the early stages of vote counting, the Oui and Non votes were running dead even. As the evening wore on, however, the Non votes slowly surged ahead. When the votes were finally tallied, the Non side won by a razor-thin margin of 50.4 to 49.6 percent. For the moment, Quebecers had narrowly chosen to reject sovereignty.

Yet the issues that sparked the referendum remain very much alive. Encouraged by their strong showing, sovereigntist leaders began planning for the next referendum. As Parizeau told fellow Francophones shortly after the 1995 referendum,

A Oui supporter, holding a Quebec flag, appeared disheartened after the Non side narrowly won the referendum.

"The next round is just around the corner, and we are going to have our country."

SIGNS OF CONFLICT

Signs of conflict continue to surface in Quebec. In an isolated incident, Francophones, upset by the fact that many stores in Montreal and Quebec City are owned and operated by English speakers, once showed their resentment by throwing bricks through the windows of English-owned stores. They've also staged protests over the employment of store clerks who don't speak French.

A few Francophones scrawled anti-Anglophone graffiti throughout Montreal after the 1995 referendum. Ted Wright, a resident of the city, photographed examples such as, "Anglos go home!" and created a poster entitled *Walls of Shame*. "The graffiti in no way represents the opinions of the majority of Francophones," the bilingual

Wright told a reporter with *Maclean's*, a Canadian weekly news magazine. In fact, this is an extreme example of anti-Anglophone behavior, and such instances happen rarely. These attitudes, though, have caused Anglophones and Allophones to leave Quebec for other parts of Canada or for the United States.

Since the referendum, sovereigntists and federalists have exchanged bitter words in Quebec's National Assembly. Federalists have challenged Quebec's need to hold another referendum and have taken the matter to federal court. Sovereigntists, on the other hand, have insisted that they will organize another referendum and that Quebec will not be bound by the decisions of "foreign courts." Premier Bouchard has warned federalists that Quebec's National Assembly will unilaterally declare independence if the national government tries to interfere with Quebec's desire to decide its own future status within Canada.

The war over Quebec's language laws also continues to raise tempers. For more than a decade, Francophones have sought to protect the dominant status of their language in Quebec by restricting the use of English in government, business, and industry. For example, according to one law, business owners who display English-only signs (or signs in which English is more prominent than French) are subject to fines. In 1996 PQ **hard-liners** tried, without success, to revoke Bill 86, the law that allows bilingual French-English commercial signs in Quebec. A hard-line victory would have made the use of English on many signs illegal.

But to win the battle over Bill 86, Premier Bouchard had to compromise. He ensured hard-line Francophones that his government would more aggressively enforce existing language laws and restore the Committee to Protect the French Language. This group of inspectors,

Anti-Anglophone graffiti appeared on this Protestant church in Montreal shortly after the referendum. Such graffiti conveyed the anger and frustration felt by some members of Quebec's Francophone community.

> *"For every isolated piece of political graffiti, brick thrown through a bookstore window, or conflict involving unilingual store clerks, people in these regions can provide a thousand daily examples of mutual cooperation and respect."*
>
> A reporter for *Maclean's*

called the "language police" by many Anglophones, reports violations of Quebec's language laws and sometimes even fines those who violate language laws on commercial signs.

On November 30, 1998, Quebecers went to the polls to vote in a provincial election that many observers considered crucial to the future of the sovereigntist cause. Prior to the vote, Quebec premier Lucien Bouchard promised his supporters that, if reelected, his Parti Québécois would sponsor a third referendum on Quebec sovereignty, proba-

bly in the year 2001. Bouchard's opponent, Liberal Party member Jean Charest, said there would be no referendum if he were elected premier.

It was a very close race. Bouchard and the PQ lost the **popular vote** by a thin margin—42.8 percent to the federalist's 43.6 percent—but they won a majority of seats in the Quebec National Assembly. These results ensured Bouchard's reelection as Quebec's premier.

But Quebecers surprised Bouchard when 70 percent voted against holding

another referendum anytime soon. With sovereigntist leadership, however, Quebecers can expect the debate over the province's future to continue. If the past is a prologue to the future, the next referendum—should there be one—might be just enough to push Quebec into sovereignty.

EFFECT ON DAILY LIVES

Many Francophones in Quebec live in small cities and towns that are almost exclusively French. These people rarely, if ever, encounter Anglophones or Allophones. Most of Quebec's newspapers and television and radio stations supply news in French. Many of the films shown at theaters are in French, too. Teachers in the public school system teach predominantly in French, including at Quebec's three French universities.

English language and culture is strongest in the city of Montreal and in the surrounding metropolitan area, where many English-language newspapers, magazines, and television and radio stations are based. There are three major English universities in Quebec.

Quebec Isn't the Only One

Other Canadian provinces have demanded greater control over their own affairs as well. In the early 1980s, for example, when the price of oil skyrocketed, western provinces such as Alberta began to demand more authority over their national resources. Such requests faded with the drop in oil prices during the 1990s, however.

In the Workplace

In the process of setting up a website for his small computer company, marketing director Scott Robinson inserted a Canadian flag beside his firm's addresses in Montreal and Toronto and French and U.S. flags next to the branches in those countries. A fellow Francophone worker saw the web page and suggested he place a Quebec flag next to the Montreal office instead.

When Robinson disagreed, a calm but intense debate ensued over which flag would be more appropriate—the Canadian maple leaf or the Quebec fleur-de-lis. "I didn't take it as an insult, but it's anti-Canadian and I wasn't going to accept it," Robinson told a reporter with *The Globe & Mail.* "Everybody thinks they're neutral and the others are biased." Such routine exchanges highlight the day-to-day differences that still divide Quebecers who favor sovereignty from those who are for federalism.

Parents whose first language is English can send their children to one of the province's many English-language public schools. With a few exceptions, however, Quebec requires Francophone and Allophone children to attend French-language public schools. Allophone parents, therefore, must send their children to French public schools, unless they can afford English private schools. Although all students in French schools study English from fourth grade on, this law is a sore point among Allophones. They want their children to be schooled in English, the primary language of social, economic, and cultural affairs in North America.

Despite their differences on the independence issue, the majority of Quebecers are committed to resolving their disagreements in a peaceful manner. In many parts of Quebec, Francophones, Anglophones, and Allophones live, work, and interact with one another every day. In Montreal, the Eastern Townships, and the Ottawa Valley—places where Anglophones and Francophones have the most interaction—moderate Quebecers have achieved not only peaceful coexistence but also a rich blending of cultures.

THE FUTURE

Meanwhile, political parties on both sides of the conflict are scrambling to win over moderate Francophones who voted Non in the 1995 referendum. The federalists, led by the Liberal Party, are trying to put together a unity package that appeals to these moderates. At the same time, sovereigntist parties remain convinced that sovereignty is necessary. They hope to persuade moderate Francophone voters that sovereignty is the only answer for Quebec.

Future elections in Canada and Quebec will shape the next chapter in the conflict over independence, but how did Quebecers get to this point? To begin to understand the conflict, it helps to take a look at Quebec's history. And the roots of tension in Quebec extend back to the stormy relationship between the Francophones and Anglophones who fought for power and control of the province more than 200 years ago. ⊕

2

THE CONFLICT'S ROOTS

Long before European explorers and adventurers set foot in North America, indigenous peoples inhabited the area that came to be known as Quebec. By the 1500s, groups who spoke Algonquian languages—such as the Algonquin and Micmac—hunted, fished, and gathered berries in Quebec's eastern woodlands. The Cree, another Algonquian group, lived in northern Quebec. Those who spoke Iroquoian languages, including the Huron and the Iroquois, lived in the lowlands along the St. Lawrence River. A third group, the Inuit people, lived in Quebec's far north, along the shores of Hudson Bay and Ungava Bay.

NEWCOMERS

In 1534 King Francis I of France commissioned Jacques Cartier to look for gold and

Jacques Cartier, credited with the European discovery of Canada, was also the first European to chart the St. Lawrence River.

to discover a new trade route to Asia. Cartier, a seasoned navigator and explorer, is considered the first person to initiate the modern Euro-

pean colonization of Canada. Cartier and his crew of 60 men set sail aboard two ships in April 1534. In early May, Cartier landed on what came to be called the Gaspé Peninsula and claimed the area for France.

Cartier and his crew then sailed back to France but returned to the Gulf of St. Lawrence in the summer of 1535. This time Cartier's expedition traveled up the St. Lawrence River, eventually reaching the Huron village of Hochelaga, the site of present-day Montreal. Cartier established the area as part of New France, the name France gave its colony. While Cartier and his men did not find precious minerals or a trade route to Asia, his trip did mark the beginning of France's interest in North America. Cartier also paved the way for future French explorers.

ABITATION DE QVEBECQ

The Quebec Habitation, France's first permanent settlement in North America, was located on the site of present-day Quebec City.

For the next several decades, French settlers fished in the St. Lawrence River and traded furs with the Iroquois and Algonquin Indians who lived in the area. France, meanwhile, was embroiled in European wars and was unable to concentrate on developing New France. When these wars finally ended, France once again focused on North America.

In 1605 French explorer Samuel de Champlain set sail for North America. Like Cartier, Champlain also hoped to find gold and a trade route to Asia but failed in both missions. He did, however, establish France's first permanent settlement in North America in 1608. Champlain and his men built a trading post at an Indian village located at the spot where the St. Lawrence and Ottawa Rivers meet. This trading post, the future site of Quebec City, got its name from the Indian word *Kebek*, which means "the place where two rivers join together."

During the seventeenth century, New France grew slowly. French settlers, most of whom were seeking land and social status, came under France's **seigneurial** system. Under the seigneurial system, the French king granted land in bulk to a company, which in turn distributed it in lots to influential people called seigneurs. Seigneurs then leased individual lots to farmers called habitants. Usually from large families with a strong devotion to the Roman Catholic Church, the habitants formed a pillar of what would one day come to be known as Francophone society.

Other settlers came to New France to find their fortunes. Fur trappers, such as the *coureurs des bois*—the canoeing French of the frontier—engaged in the colony's profitable fur trade. Beaver pelts, used to make expensive top hats for fashionable Europeans, were

French trappers, known as coureurs des bois, *established a solid relationship with native Canadians. The friendly ties helped make the fur trade New France's main industry.*

interests in its American colonies, which lay south of New France. France certainly exploited its colony's wealth but also saw New France as a projection of French national pride and culture in North America. Great Britain was more clearly interested in mining the economic potential of its colonies. Meanwhile, Great Britain cast a hungry eye at France's North American holdings.

To establish a strong presence in North America, Great Britain did everything it could to encourage massive population growth in the colonies. The country sent just about anyone who could make the voyage, including convicted criminals, debtors, and other social outcasts. As a result, Britain's colonies grew much faster than France's did. By 1763 the total population of French colonists in New France was only about 65,000, compared to more than one million British colonists in North America.

In the mid-1700s, competition between France and Great Britain heated to the boiling point, eventually igniting the French and Indian

valuable commodities that could be transported easily.

FRENCH AND BRITISH RIVALRY

Great Britain and France had long been rivals. In 1066, for example, a French duke named William invaded England and became king. Almost 300 years later, the two nations clashed again when King Edward III of England claimed the French throne in what became the start of the Hundred Years' War. The competition for power and territory eventually extended into North America.

In 1670 Great Britain became interested in New France's profitable fur trade. The British established their first permanent settlement at Hudson Bay, an untouched wilderness to the north of New France. In time Great Britain's Hudson's Bay Company competed with the French fur traders for fishing and trapping rights. This ongoing rivalry led to many clashes between the British and the French, who fought with help from native Canadians.

The British Empire was focused on developing its own

War (1754–1763). At the same time, the Seven Years' War, which involved both France and Great Britain, raged in Europe.

In 1759, as part of Great Britain's plan to conquer New France, General James Wolfe attacked Quebec City. A siege lasting more than two months left the city close to ruin and its population on the verge of starvation. In a final assault, the British troops climbed a cliff during the night and attacked the French troops the next morning, when they least expected it. After a battle that lasted only 20 minutes, French forces under the command of the Marquis de Montcalm surrendered to Wolfe in a farmer's field known as the Plains of Abraham. Both Wolfe and Montcalm later died of wounds suffered in the battle. In 1760 Britain also seized control of Montreal.

When the Seven Years' War ended in 1763, France signed the Treaty of Paris, turning over its North American possessions—with the exception of the islands of St. Pierre and Miquelon—to Britain. With the stroke of a pen, New France was renamed Quebec Province, and French Québécois became British subjects.

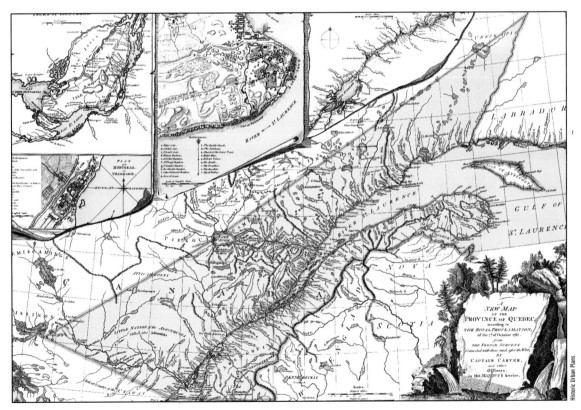

An early map of Quebec shows how the province had grown by 1763.

LIFE UNDER BRITISH RULE

Almost immediately Britain began to impose fundamental changes on its newest colony. The Royal Proclamation of 1763 redrew the boundaries of Quebec and replaced the French judicial system with English civil and criminal law. Perhaps most devastating to the French, however, was the part of the act in which Britain decreed that Quebec would be ruled by a non-elected council and an assembly, whose members were required to take an anti-Catholic oath. This meant that most French Quebecers, who were Catholic, were exempt from public office. Most of the British, on the other hand, followed the Protestant religion, so they were eligible to serve.

During this period, the province of Quebec grew and prospered, thanks in large part to a vigorous economy. French-speaking Quebecers continued to live in rural areas, where they farmed and raised animals. The Catholic Church played an increasingly central role in French lives. In contrast, most of the English-speaking Quebecers lived in Montreal and in Quebec City, where they continued to dominate trade and commerce in the province. As British subjects, merchants in Quebec could freely sell their agricultural and manufactured products to Britain, one of the largest markets in the world.

North Wind Pictures

Although the French won many of the early battles of the French and Indian War, the tide turned when British troops besieged Quebec City. France surrendered to the British after General James Wolfe and 4,500 soldiers defeated the French army on the Plains of Abraham.

QUÉBEC ACT OF 1774

In the years leading up to the American Revolution, people living in Britain's American colonies grew increasingly dissatisfied with British rule. Britain feared that this unrest might spread north to Quebec. Anticipating a possible American rebellion, the British Parliament passed the Québec Act in 1774. The goal of the Québec Act was to ensure Quebec's loyalty if a war broke out between Britain and its American colonies.

The act won Francophone support by repealing the most objectionable provisions of the Royal Proclamation of 1763. For example, it officially recognized the French language and the rights of the Roman Catholic Church. In addition, the Québec Act set up a new government, led by a governor and an appointed council, which was empowered to pass laws for the colony and to levy taxes. While English law continued to be used in criminal cases, French law once again governed civil matters. Finally, Quebec's borders were expanded as far south and west as the Mississippi and Ohio

English versus French Legal Systems

Before Britain's conquest of Quebec in 1759, the legal system in New France was based on French civil and criminal law. The French legal system, which traces its origins to ancient Roman law, is based on a written code. Judges rely on this code, which consists of general principles and rules for different types of cases, to help them decide legal questions. English common law, on the other hand, is based upon legal precedents—legal decisions made in earlier cases, particularly those made in the courts of England—rather than on statutes or laws written by a parliament or a legislature. The law is ever changing, based upon decisions made in new court cases.

To this day, Quebec's civil law is based on a written code called the *droit civil*, French for "civil law." In making legal rulings, judges first look to the droit civil and its written guidelines. They consult precedents set in earlier decisions only if and when they need further guidance. Quebec is the only one of Canada's ten provinces to use French civil law.

Rivers, thus restoring it to the former size of New France.

The provisions of the Québec Act strengthened the bond between Britain and French-speaking Quebecers just as the American colonists were preparing to rebel. By responding to the needs and interests of the French population, Britain decreased the odds of Quebec staging its own war of independence or of helping the Americans. In 1775, when American general Benedict Arnold led the Continental Army's inva-

sion of Quebec, he found no support among French Quebecers.

UPPER AND LOWER CANADA

The American colonies won their independence in 1783. However, a large group of colonists, called Loyalists, maintained their loyalty to the British crown and migrated north to Canada. This influx of English-speaking immigrants forced the British government once again to confront the fundamental ethnic and cultural divisions within its colony. These new

The act essentially split Quebec along ethnic lines. Upper Canada, the present-day province of Ontario, was predominantly inhabited by English speakers and governed by English criminal and civil law. Lower Canada, the modern-day province of Quebec, included Montreal and Quebec City.

English-speaking residents of Quebec wanted to be governed by British law and political institutions. In response, the British Parliament passed the Constitutional Act of 1791, which divided Quebec into Upper Canada and Lower Canada.

The act essentially split Quebec along ethnic lines. Upper Canada, the present-day province of Ontario, was predominantly inhabited by English speakers and was governed by English criminal and civil law. Lower Canada, the modern-day province of Quebec, included Montreal and Quebec City. The bulk of Quebec's French-speaking population and a smaller group of English speakers resided in this area. Over time, however, English influence—especially in business—grew in Lower Canada.

The Constitutional Act of 1791 established a system of representative government in both Upper and Lower Canada and gave women the right to own property. The act created an assembly elected by local voters and two additional governing bodies—a legislative council and an executive council.

But the new arrangement was flawed from the start. Britain appointed two governors—one to oversee affairs in Upper Canada and another to rule Lower Canada. In turn, each of these governors appointed members to serve on the legislative and executive councils. And, because the act did not specifically determine the balance of power between the branches of government, the executive branch could not be made to carry out the wishes of the legislative assembly. The governors and the appointed councils were responsible to the government in Britain rather than to the assembly and the people. Thus the elected assembly was in many ways little more than a forum for airing grievances.

The framers of the act had been reluctant to address the language issue directly. Perhaps it was not surprising, then, that the issue surfaced at the very first meeting of the Lower Canada assembly, which met in Quebec City in 1792. Lawmakers debated the future status of the French language and the importance of its preservation. Although French had no official status within Quebec, government documents had been printed in both French and English following the British conquest in 1763. Francophone legislators wanted to sanction French legally, while Anglophones insisted on maintaining English as the sole official language. In the end, legislators decreed that both languages were official. The British Parliament in London, however, overturned this compromise, making English the province's only official language.

RISE OF FRENCH-CANADIAN NATIONALISM

From the very beginning of representative government in Lower Canada, there was a split between Anglophone and Francophone legislators. Since British-appointed governors chose all council members, the English speakers dominated both the executive and legislative councils. The most powerful Anglophone politicians, who controlled the executive branch of government, were called the Château Clique, named after the governor's residence.

Francophone political strength was concentrated in the House of Assembly. The most powerful Francophone group to oppose the Château Clique were the Patriotes—also called the Popular Party or Radicals. The Patriotes were led by the charismatic Louis-Joseph Papineau, Speaker of the House of Assembly.

The Château Clique and the Patriotes disagreed on many major economic and constitutional issues. In particular, they locked horns over the relationship between the legislative and executive branches of government. Papineau and his followers argued that the executive branch of government, led by the governor, should be made responsible to the legislative branch.

The Anglophones strongly objected to these demands. If the executive branch was responsible to the Assembly, they feared, French-speaking Quebecers would gain the upper hand in the government and legislate French supremacy in Quebec. Anglophones in Quebec City—Quebec's leading commercial and industrial center at the time—also thought that the French lacked business sense and feared that Francophone domination would hurt or delay Quebec's economic growth. So Anglophone lawmakers refused to address the demands put forth by Papineau and the Patriotes.

This conflict escalated during the 1830s. The Patriotes, inspired by Francophone radicals and by extremists in the United States, became increasingly

National Archives of Canada/C395

By the 1830s, tension between French and English Canadians had escalated. When the English-dominated executive and legislative councils dismissed Francophone concerns, the Patriotes rose in revolt.

agitated about the need for change. Hit hard by weather- and disease-induced crop failures, the Patriotes responded strongly to Papineau's inflammatory rhetoric. Papineau pushed them to organize public rallies and boycotts against what he called the dominance of "loathsome and insufferable" English aristocrats. Eventually the continued unrest and economic hardship led to an armed struggle. In late 1837 and again in 1838, Patriotes battled against British troops near Montreal. But the British quickly defeated the ill-equipped Patriotes.

Sir Francis Bond Head, the governor-general of Upper Canada, ordered British troops to arrest the rebels. The Patriotes were later tried in British-controlled courts and were sentenced to long prison terms. Some of the rebels were even executed. Although the rebellions

Louis-Joseph Papineau was the first politician to articulate the concerns of Canada's Francophone population.

Archives Nationales du Quebec a Quebec/Aubert et Cie

Louis-Joseph Papineau: Distinguished Patriote or Reluctant Rebel?

Louis-Joseph Papineau was born in Montreal in 1786 to a distinguished French family. His father, Joseph Papineau, was a member of Quebec's French nobility and was a descendant of the original settlers who came to New France in the 1670s. Joseph Papineau was an elected representative in Lower Canada's House of Assembly, the legislative body established by the Constitutional Act of 1791. Louis-Joseph, like his father, was a staunch nationalist and a strong defender of the French language.

Louis-Joseph began his political career at the early age of 20, when he won a seat representing the county of Kent. He became a lawyer in 1810 and later served with distinction as an officer in the French militia during the War of 1812. At the end of the war, he took over his father's seat in the House of Assembly, representing the county of East Montreal.

In the House of Assembly, Louis-Joseph quickly developed a reputation as one of the most outspoken and intelligent advocates of French-speaking Canadians. From 1815 to 1823 and again from 1825 to 1832, he served as Speaker of the House of Assembly.

Papineau had a complicated personality. In religious matters, he was considered a "freethinker," someone who did not blindly follow the dictates of the Roman Catholic Church. Yet Quebec's wealthy citizens, like the Papineaus, tended to be conservative. While Papineau often used dramatic rhetoric to failed to achieve the Patriotes' objectives, the struggle played an important role in the future of the French-English conflict. The resounding Francophone defeat led most Francophones to abandon armed revolt as an acceptable political strategy. Instead, the reform movement channeled its energy into the political process, hoping to achieve change through legislative action.

THE DURHAM REPORT

Although the British government effectively suppressed the outbreaks, the Rebellion of 1837 marked the depth of division between the English and French populations in the region. Britain commissioned a special board of inquiry to look into the causes of the rebellion. A noble named John George Lambton, Earl of Durham, led the board of inquiry.

In the Durham Report, issued in 1839, Lord Durham sided with the Patriotes' demand for responsible government by agreeing that the legislature should control the executive branch of government. Yet his report also criticized French society for being "old and stationary. . . in a new and progressive world." He recommended assimilating French-speaking Quebec by uniting Upper and Lower Canada into one province. Durham urged Britain to establish a single legislature for the new Province of Canada. He also maximized Quebec's self-government of internal matters, leaving Britain to control the province's external affairs.

In 1840 Britain responded to Durham's report by passing the Act of Union. The measure merged the territories of Lower Canada (which was to be called Canada

inspire followers and to blast his opponents, he had difficulty making decisions and taking action.

Throughout the 1820s and 1830s, Papineau became the chief opponent of an English plan to reunite Upper and Lower Canada. He earned lasting fame as a leading member of the Patriotes. His party openly denounced the power and privileges of Anglophone bureaucrats in Lower Canada's ruling Château Clique. Specifically, Papineau and his fellow Patriotes accused the Anglophones of using government power for their own private gain.

In 1834 Papineau made a historic speech in the Assembly when he presented the Ninety-Two Resolutions, a comprehensive list of grievances of the people in Lower Canada. Britain responded three years later with the Russell Resolutions. This list of 10 directives instructed Quebec's governor to reject Papineau's call for reform and to defy the House of Assembly, if necessary, to maintain order.

While Papineau was outraged at Britain's response, he counseled moderation to his supporters. Yet it was too late. Confronted with this final British insult and a sagging agricultural economy, the French were ready for rebellion. Although Papineau did not join the Rebellion of 1837, the government issued a warrant for his arrest. Papineau fled to Vermont and later lived in Paris, France. After a grant of amnesty, Papineau returned to Quebec and was later reelected to the Parliament of United Canada in January 1848. He retired from politics in 1854 and died on September 23, 1871, at age 85.

Archives Nationales du Quebec a Quebec/M. Desnoyers

Francophone leader Louis-Hippolyte LaFontaine believed that the divisions between English and French Canadians could be settled by a responsible government that answered to the people rather than to the privileged elite.

East) and Upper Canada (called Canada West) into a single colony with one parliament. The act granted both territories equal representation in an elected assembly. By providing for equal representation in the House of Assembly, however, the act effectively dis-criminated against the much larger French Canadian population in Canada East. Francophones objected to this arrangement because it gave the smaller English population of Canada East the same political clout as the French majority.

The Act of Union was a disappointment to most Francophones. It did not create the responsible government that Papineau and the Patriotes had fought so hard to achieve. In addition, Article 41 of the act made English the only official language of a united Canada, stripping French Canadians of language rights that had been guaranteed to them in the Québec Act of 1774. Louis-Hippolyte LaFontaine, who had risen to become a strong leader among Francophones, vigorously protested this provision. But aside from the language issue, LaFontaine supported a united Canada. He felt that Francophones would have the best chance to secure peace and prosperity in a united Canada, one where distinctions based on ethnicity had been eliminated.

During this time, which came to be known as the Period of Union, moderate reformers in Canada West and Canada East joined to establish the Reform Party. Led by LaFontaine and Robert Baldwin, an English Canadian, the Reform Party was the first effective coalition of French and English political leadership in Canada. Together LaFontaine and Baldwin won national elections in 1847. As leaders of a joint administration, LaFontaine and Baldwin had the power to make responsible government a reality.

In the same year, the British appointed Lord Elgin as the new governor-general of a unified Canada. Elgin disagreed with Durham's assessment that French Canadians should be denied language rights. In 1848 he argued to repeal Article 41 and to restore the language rights of French Canadians. The British government agreed with Elgin and repealed the article, making the Province of Canada bilingual once more.

BRITISH NORTH AMERICA ACT

The middle of the nineteenth century was a period of rapid economic growth for Canada West and Canada East. Developers laid railroads from Montreal to Canada West and the United States. New canals on the St. Lawrence River enabled ships to get around rapids, opening up the waterway from the Atlantic Ocean through to the Great Lakes. By the 1860s, however, Canada was still a politically divided country. And its building spree had created a huge debt. The British Parliament offered little help. In fact, Britain's attention seemed to be too focused on consolidating its territories in British North America to counter the growing economic strength of the United States, its former colony to the south. By pulling together the British colonies into a **confederation,** British politicians hoped to retain their influence in North America.

Under the terms of the proposed confederation, Canada East, Canada West, Nova Scotia, and New Brunswick would be united as the **Dominion** of Canada. Canada East would become Quebec Province, and Canada West would become Ontario Province. This new political arrangement guaranteed the use of the French language in Quebec and Quebec's autonomy in educational and other local

In 1866 delegates from Upper Canada, Lower Canada, New Brunswick, and Novia Scotia met in Ontario to discuss forming a confederation. Supporters of confederation believed that it would help solve the economic problems facing the Canadian colonies. Francophone supporters believed that confederation would enable French Canadians to regain their provincial identity.

Confederation Life Insurance Company

matters. The confederation made the province of Quebec officially bilingual.

In Canada's four provinces, legislators made many arguments both for and against confederation. Francophones wanted to make sure that provinces would be represented in the new Canadian parliament in proportion to their population. Anglophones in Quebec, who were in the minority, wanted to ensure that they had an equally strong voice in deciding their political destiny. Although a vigorous debate ensued, supporters of confederation vastly outnumbered those against it, and the confederation became a reality under the British North America Act of 1867.

Despite having to answer to the British monarch, the new dominion had a central government—headquartered in Ottawa, Ontario—with power to regulate some of the nation's affairs. The provinces could also decide some things on their own. Yet the Ottawa government, controlled by Britain, still appointed all provincial governors and was able to veto any laws passed by provincial legislatures. Any powers not specifically granted to the provinces were reserved for the federal government. Canadians could not modify their new constitution in any way.

Although the act made some concessions to French interests, the federal government retained much authority. This situation failed to erase fears that English-speaking Canadians would dominate Quebec politically. It also preserved the status of Canadians as British subjects—a title that French Quebecers disliked.

REBELLIONS IN THE WEST

Just as many Francophones had feared, Anglophone conservatives controlled the national government in Ottawa. Their policies stirred resentment, not only among Canadians from several ethnic groups living within the Dominion's boundaries, but also among groups farther west. Like the United States, Canada had begun to push westward, seizing territory along the way. The new settlers encountered resistance from the people inhabiting these areas. The native groups on the western plains were angry at whites, who had destroyed their way of life by creating farms and towns. The Métis (people of mixed French and Indian ancestry who lived in what would become Saskatchewan and Manitoba) were upset that the English-led government ignored their land claims.

By 1869 the Métis were ready to fight. Louis Riel, a well-educated and charismatic French-speaking Métis, led his people in a revolt at the group's Red

Facing Page: *Louis Riel (center) defends himself during his trial. The revolt led by Riel and his supporters made Riel a hero among French Canadians. Outraged Francophones criticized French-speaking members of Parliament for not speaking out against his execution.*

River Settlement (in present-day Manitoba). British troops crushed the rebellion, and Riel, who had become a hero to the French-speaking people, fled. The Métis moved farther west to farm along the Saskatchewan River. But by 1885, the Dominion government had entered Métis lands once again. Louis Riel staged another armed uprising that came to be known as the North-West Rebellion. At a secret meeting held beforehand, Riel and a group of prominent Métis had signed an oath to "save their country from a wicked government by taking up arms if necessary." Two weeks later, Riel and his followers seized a church in Saskatchewan, formed a provisional government, and demanded the surrender of Fort Carlton, the key to control over the territory.

The event was a disaster for the Métis. Government troops quickly squelched the uprising and captured Riel and several of his fellow conspirators. A British-controlled court found Riel guilty of high treason and sentenced him to death by hanging. Others received prison terms. Riel's execution created strong resentment among French Canadians who had lobbied on his behalf. They considered him a martyr and a defender of the rights of the French speakers in western Canada. Riel's execution seemed to confirm French-Canadian fears that they were essentially powerless in a united Canada.

National Archives of Canada/C1879

Following Riel's death, there was limited improvement in the fortunes of French Canadians. In 1896 Sir Wilfred Laurier, a prominent lawyer who had supported Riel's position, won national elections to become the first French-Canadian prime minister of Canada. The leader of the Liberal Party, Laurier also began Quebec's long-running support of that party.

Prime Minister Wilfred Laurier's decision to send Canadian volunteers to support Britain in South Africa's Boer War angered many French Canadians.

National Archives of Canada/PA13153

FALLING BEHIND

Meanwhile, even though the industrial revolution had hit Ontario, and business in Montreal was thriving due to the city's prime location on the St. Lawrence Seaway, Quebec's overall economy and services lagged behind. Busy with developing the western provinces, the national government left Quebec's educational systems and health care needs to the Catholic Church. Furthermore, the church encouraged many French-speaking Canadians to preserve their culture by continuing to farm their small pieces of land in rural Quebec. The old French tradition of giving sections of the family plot to sons and grandsons eventu-ally created farms too small to support future generations. Although the church warned Francophones of the dangers of city living, the lack of sufficient land forced young people to take low-paying manufacturing jobs in urban areas. Some people decided to leave Canada to look for work in U.S. cities.

Laurier and other moderate Francophone leaders urged French Canadians to seek their fortunes within a united Canada. The provin-cial government joined the Catholic Church in trying to convince the French Canadians to stay in the country. The government gave French Canadians farmland on the Gaspé Peninsula, while the church set up programs to open up and settle new farming areas.

DIVIDED IN WAR

The gap between French and English Canadians had widened significantly by the time Britain entered

World War I (1914–1918) in September 1914. Because Canada was a member of the **British Commonwealth,** most Canadians and most British assumed that Canada was also at war. Yet many Francophones had a different view. As they had in 1898, when Britain sent troops to South Africa to fight in the Boer War, Francophones strongly objected to sending their sons to fight and die for the British in a foreign war where Canada's security was not at stake. Leading Quebec legislators such as Henri Bourassa angrily denounced plans to enlist French-speaking Quebecers in Britain's war effort.

As the death toll in World War I mounted, military recruiters found it increasingly difficult to meet Canada's commitment to providing troops for the war effort.

Father Lionel Groulx, an ardent Francophone nationalist and founder of the magazine *L'Action Française,* was also an ardent anti-Semite and a racist. Groulx's views tainted the Francophone cause. Because of Groulx's influence, many people still associate the sovereignty movement with intolerance and bigotry.

As a result, the Canadian government began to draft young Canadian men into military service. The **conscription** policy meant that Francophones would serve under British commanders. Riots and protests over the draft erupted in Quebec City, causing a major crisis. Many young French-speaking Quebecers went into hiding to avoid going to war. Quebec was nearly unanimous in its opposition to the draft. This stance further separated the French-speaking province from the rest of Canada, which had no problem with sending recruits to fight for the British.

Continuing conflicts over language heightened French-Canadian protests against the draft. Just before the war, French speakers in Ontario had been angered by Regulation 17, a law making it illegal for schools to teach in French beyond the second grade. Francophones also had a difficult time in the Canadian armed forces, where the English language was dominant and where few officers spoke French.

By 1917 Quebec had been alienated from the rest of Canada. In that year, a group of young intellectuals led by Father Lionel Groulx founded a monthly journal called *L'Action Française.* These idealistic young priests, lawyers, and journalists regarded Quebec as the only viable stronghold of French culture and of the Roman Catholic Church in Canada. They dreamed of the day when Quebec would be free of British rule.

> "If we must fight for our freedom, we must stay here. I am saying, and I do not care where my comments are repeated, that any French Canadian who enlists is not doing his duty."
>
> Armand Lavergne
> a leader in Quebec's fight against the draft

Although popular during World War I, this message had less appeal for French Canadians after the fighting had ended. Producing goods for the war effort had given Quebec's economy a much needed boost. Relative prosperity left the majority of French Canadians feeling satisfied with the status quo. But the political solidarity that had developed among Francophones during the war years remained intact.

RISING NATIONALISM

By 1920 Quebec was ready to catch the second wave of the industrial revolution. A hydroelectric dam built just north of Trois-Rivières on the St. Maurice River produced enough power to run the paper mills and other industries that soon sprouted nearby. In northwestern Quebec, gold and copper mines provided jobs. But the province's economic good fortune ended abruptly when the winter-wheat crop failed in 1928. The economic depression that soon engulfed all of Canada sparked another upsurge in Quebec nationalism.

In 1936 voters elected Maurice Duplessis—a member of the newly formed and highly conservative Union Nationale party—as premier of Quebec. Duplessis won the election on a pledge to work for social reform and to clean up corrupt British-dominated commercial

National Archives of Canada/C.M. Johnston/PA56874

When the depression of the 1930s brought the wood, paper, and textile industries to a standstill, unemployment and homelessness soared in Quebec.

A crowd of Quebecers gathers at an anticonscription rally in Montreal during World War II. The drafting of Canadians created tension between Anglophones and Francophones, as it had during World War I.

trusts in Quebec. Yet his administration became known for stuffing ballot boxes and for extorting money from corporations to stay in office. In addition, Duplessis's administration left behind a legacy of **provincialism** that embittered many Anglophones and Allophones in Quebec.

The deep divide between French and English Canadians resurfaced when World War II broke out in 1939. While both Francophones and Anglophones eventually supported participation in the Allied cause, the French understanding was that, for the most part, Canada would provide economic support, and that Canadian military service would be strictly voluntary. Even though voters rejected the Union Nationale party in 1939 elections— largely because the party was opposed to Quebec's participation in the war—the conflict over whether to enact conscription escalated.

As the war dragged on and the Allies needed more soldiers, the Canadian government asked Canadian citizens to allow a draft. Once again the vote revealed a major split between French- and English-speaking Canadians. While 80 percent of Anglophones voted yes, 72 percent of Francophones said no. When the Canadian prime minister ordered 16,000 draftees into service in November 1944, major riots and demonstrations

CHAPTER 2 *The Conflict's Roots*

broke out in the streets of Quebec. At some military bases, Francophones came close to mutiny.

Meanwhile, the same war that angered so many Quebecers sent the province's economy into overdrive. In Quebec workers refined the aluminum used to build airplanes and other wartime machinery. Other industries boomed, such as textile manufacturing, chemical production, and the processing of food items.

In August 1944, however, Quebecers who had been angry about the war reelected Duplessis as Quebec's premier. During the next 15 years, the Union Nationale government modernized Quebec. Crews built roads and bridges and provided electricity to rural areas. In 1948 Duplessis made the French fleur-de-lis the province's official symbol, and Quebec established its own corporate and personal income taxes. Duplessis's conservative, probusiness philosophy helped spur economic growth and foreign investment in Quebec. At the same time, he spent more money on roads and bridges than he did on education or on health and welfare. The Duplessis administration was also widely known to be corrupt, relying on old ties with the Catholic Church and its business interests. Duplessis publicized that he was highly suspicious of the English-speaking federal government, contributing to Quebec's continuing conflict with the rest of Canada.

THE GAP WIDENS

During the 1940s and 1950s, the divide between French- and English-speaking Quebecers persisted. Anglophones tended to live in large urban areas such as Montreal and its surrounding cities and towns. Most of Quebec's business and industrial leaders were Anglophones, and they dominated the political and economic life of the province. Because most large companies did business in English, knowing the language was a vital economic asset. English schools offered students practical training for business and industry.

On the other hand, the vast majority of French Quebecers still lived in rural areas, where they supported themselves by farming or fishing. The Roman Catholic Church continued to be the

In 1944 Maurice Duplessis returned to power on the strength of anticonscription sentiment. During Duplessis's second tenure as prime minister, the economy of Quebec thrived, but tension between the province and the rest of Canada grew.

dominant institution in their lives. French schools, largely controlled by the church, provided a classical education with an emphasis on language and culture, leaving many Francophones unprepared for careers in a modern, industrial economy.

By 1959 more than half of the Francophone population had not completed grade school, and only two percent of high school graduates went on to attend colleges, universities, or other post-secondary institutions. Francophone workers typically earned less than did Anglophones who held similar jobs.

In many ways, English-speaking Canadians regarded French speakers as ignorant peasants and treated them as second-class citizens. Francophones often worked for Anglophone bosses who didn't speak French. Government services were usually provided exclusively in English. Although a few notable Francophones achieved significant economic and political status, most were stuck on the bottom rung of society. Quebec's French-speaking majority, angry about its lack of political and eco-

A Shift in Nationalism

The meaning of French-Canadian nationalism—the collective will of French-speaking Canadians to live as a cultural community apart from English-speaking Canadians—changed over time. The French-Canadian nationalism of the 1700s and early 1800s was a response to the British conquest of New France and to economic hardship. This earliest version aimed to preserve traditional lifestyles. The Catholic Church, at the center of this way of life, promoted agricultural careers and the preservation of French culture and language among the Québécois.

By the end of World War II in 1945, however, economic and political themes came to dominate nationalism among French Canadians. The postwar influx of European immigrants made Quebec more diverse, and the industrial age forever changed the province's economic landscape. As a result, the Québécois focused on uniting all of Quebec's citizens under the banner of building a better economy and making the province a more pleasant place in which to live.

The Quiet Revolution of the 1960s ushered in a wave of aggressive nationalism among Québécois. During that time, the province gained control over issues that had been in the hands of the federal government—its natural resources, such as hydroelectric power, and its social services. These drastic changes prompted the Québécois to search for a common thread that could be used to bind together the people of the province. The French language became this thread, and the Québécois went to great lengths to enforce the language laws.

nomic influence, was ready for reform.

When Maurice Duplessis died suddenly in 1959, Francophones got the opportunity to make big changes. Without a strong leader waiting in the wings,

the Union Nationale party lost momentum. In the 1960 elections, Jean Lesage of Quebec's Liberal Party became the new premier, beginning a period of reform that came to be known as the Quiet Revolution. ⊕

3

THE PRESENT CONFLICT

The Quiet Revolution involved a dramatic transformation of Quebec's political, social, and economic institutions. Although Lesage was a committed federalist, he encouraged Francophones to be proud of their history and culture and sought to make French the dominant language in Quebec. Lesage and other leading Francophone politicians and intellectuals recognized that Quebec had developed a modern industrial economy and that its French-speaking society needed to catch up with the rest of Canada and North America.

During the Quiet Revolution, Francophones rebelled against the influence of the Roman Catholic Church and adopted a more **secular** identity defined by French language and culture. They began to view provincial government as an agent they could use to protect French-Canadian culture and to help Quebec grow economically. Under this philosophy, Quebec took on many services that had previously been provided by the federal government. One of the first changes Quebecers made was to reform the school system. Long under the control of the Catholic Church, French-language schools lagged behind English-language institutions. So the provincial government took charge of education. Quebec's government also exercised more authority over the province's industrial resources—including Hydro-Québec, Canada's leading producer of electricity—which until then had been managed by the federal government.

Francophones rebelled against the Anglophone economic elite that still dominated commerce at that time. In a period of social, political, and economic change, provincial courts revised labor laws, giving Quebecers the right to strike

Jean Lesage's reforms modernized Quebec but also made Francophones more aware of the differences between their province and the rest of Canada.

AP/Wide World Photos

for higher wages and benefits. The provincial government also focused on economic growth and on providing the practical business and technical training necessary to help young Francophones enter the middle class.

FRANCOPHONE PRIDE

The renewed strength of Francophone interests in the province encouraged French speakers to seek more protections for their culture and language. French-speaking Quebecers, for example, insisted that the term "Québécois" be used to replace the term "French Canadian." The most telling change was the support the growing Francophone middle class gave to the sovereigntist movement. And voters had several organizations to choose from. These new groups spanned the political spectrum from extreme left to extreme right, but all encouraged Québécois to push for independence from Canada.

As could be expected, these developments increased tensions with English speakers in Quebec and in the rest of Canada. Support for independence had not yet become

The Sovereigntist Movement Takes Root

Two sovereigntist groups—the Mouvement Souveraineté-Association (MSA) and the Rassemblement pour l'indépendence National (RIN)—merged in 1968 to form the Parti Québécois (PQ). The PQ was responsible for bringing an acceptable version of the independence message to a majority of the Quebec electorate. The PQ gained support rapidly, and by 1976 it had won provincial elections.

widespread—not even among Francophones. In fact, in the early 1960s, when Quebecers first responded to a poll asking if Quebec should separate from Canada, only about 10 percent of the population favored the idea. Approximately 75 percent of Francophones opposed independence.

Later in the decade, however, the sovereigntist movement slowly gained ground. In 1962 Lesage and the Liberal Party rode to reelection on the slogan "Masters in our own home." A year later, in 1963, the Front de Libération du Québec (FLQ) expressed the dark side of sovereigntism when it claimed responsibility for a wave of terrorist bombings. FLQ members placed bombs in the mailboxes of three federal armories in Westmount, a wealthy Anglo-

phone area of Montreal. In 1964, when the British monarch visited Canada to celebrate a century of confederation, sovereigntists viewed the queen's arrival as a provocation. Sovereigntist demonstrators in Quebec City booed the queen, even though she had been invited by Quebec's provincial government. Municipal police subdued an angry group of student protestors with clubs. During the same year, the FLQ held up a Canadian company called International Firearms, stealing $50,000 in cash and weapons and killing the company vice president.

LANGUAGE RIGHTS

In 1965 Lester Pearson, Canada's prime minister, established the first Royal Commission on Bilingualism and Biculturalism. The goal

In 1964 sovereigntists in Quebec City protested the visit of Queen Elizabeth, holding up signs that said, "Death to Anglo-Canadian racism."

of the commission was to identify and resolve some of the problems and challenges created by Canada's dual-language identity. In a report delivered in 1967, the commission noted that French- and English-speaking Quebecers were deeply divided.

French speakers had long felt shut out of Canadian society. At times English-language dominance left Francophones at a dangerous disadvantage. Elderly Francophones, for example, had

died in nursing homes where English was the only language spoken. In a less urgent but famous incident, a clerk at an English department store in Montreal demanded that a Francophone "speak white" when asking a question.

There was a sense of urgency behind the campaign for French-language rights, fueled by two trends that threatened French culture in Quebec. First, Francophone birthrates in Quebec had fallen sharply, eroding Francophone political power and

influence in the province. In past years, the highly influential Catholic Church had encouraged couples to have many children, giving Quebec the highest birthrate in Canada and one of the highest birthrates in the industrialized world. As the Catholic Church fell out of favor, however, Quebec society had become more urbanized. The middle class had grown, but the number of Francophone births had plunged. By the late 1960s, Quebec had gone from having the highest provincial birthrate in the country to having the lowest.

The second alarming trend was the influx of new immigrants that had flowed steadily into Quebec since 1945. Almost one million people from countries such as Italy, Greece, Hungary, Germany, Armenia, Czechoslovakia (modern Slovakia and the Czech Republic), and Portugal had moved to Quebec to escape economic hardship. Most of these immigrants had settled in Montreal, Toronto, and other cities. In Quebec the dramatic growth of the Allophone population had reduced the relative percentage of the French population. And most of these new immigrants wanted their children to attend English-language schools. In 1968, in the Montreal suburb of St. Leonard, a major fight over language rights erupted. Angry parents protested when the suburb's Catholic school board voted to deny English-language education to a group of mostly Italian immigrants.

The St. Leonard incident prompted the provincial legislature to pass a law that granted immigrants the right to choose English-language or French-language schools for their children. The law seemed to satisfy newcomers. But many Francophones grew more determined than ever to fight for language rights in a province where they still formed a strong majority. They argued that if Montreal became exclusively English speaking, so would the rest of Quebec, because half of the province's population, and almost two-thirds of its industries, were based in the Montreal area.

Meanwhile, the FLQ had stepped up its tactics, using larger and more powerful weapons in its prosovereignty campaign. In 1968 the group detonated bombs at McGill University and at the Montreal Stock Exchange. The bombs injured 27 people.

French Faux Pas

On an official visit to Canada in 1967, Canada's centennial year, French President Charles de Gaulle *(below)* raised his arms in a victory salute and shouted *Vive le Québec libre!* ("Long live free Quebec!") from the balcony of the Montreal City Hall. The Canadian government denounced the remark. It regarded the remark as outside interference in Canada's internal affairs. De Gaulle quickly left the country, deciding to skip a scheduled meeting with Canada's leaders in Ottawa. His visit chilled Canada's relationship with France for 20 years.

UPI/Corbis-Bettmann

During the 1960s, the dispute over language and culture grew violent. In 1963 the prosovereignty FLQ planted a mail bomb that killed a Montreal police officer (right). In the 1968 St. Leonard riots (below), immigrants battled with police over the right to have their children attend English-language schools.

CP Picture Archive/The Gazette Montreal

THE LANGUAGE LAWS

During the same year, under the leadership of Canada's newly elected prime minister, Pierre Elliot Trudeau, Francophones in Quebec began to win some important legal victories for language rights. A bilingual Quebecer regarded as one of Canada's most brilliant leaders, Trudeau was committed to bridging the gap between Anglophones and Francophones. In 1968 the Royal Commission on Bilingualism and Biculturalism recommended that all Canadian children be required to study French—Canada's unofficial second language. In 1969 another commission

The Gazette, Montreal

stressed the importance of preserving Canada's distinct French and English heritages.

Trudeau supported equal language rights for French- and English-speaking Canadians when he backed the Official Languages Act in 1969. The law made French one of Canada's two official languages and ensured that Francophones had equal access to federal government jobs and services throughout Canada. Legislators hoped that the act would also help to unify Canada and to reduce sovereigntist pressure.

While many Francophones cheered the passage of the Official Languages Act, the law did not end the conflict over language rights. Quebec's Francophone leaders pushed to make French the province's dominant language of government, commerce, and culture—areas where English had always been more widespread.

THE GROWING DIVIDE

Meanwhile, in October 1970, the FLQ captured headlines around the world by kidnapping James Cross, a British trade commissioner, and killing Pierre LaPorte, a Quebec cabinet minister.

During what became known as the October Crisis, Trudeau called in the army and invoked the War Measures Act. The act suspended the civil liberties of Quebecers and allowed the government to step in and stop the violence. Police quickly arrested and detained 465 people, most of whom had nothing to do with the kidnapping and who were never charged with a crime. The heavy-handed response led to the breakup of

the FLQ in 1971. But it also upset moderate Quebecers who sympathized with the FLQ's aims, if not with its tactics. The crackdown fueled a strong antifederalist backlash among Francophones who already didn't trust Canada's federal government.

The Trudeau administration's controversial response during the October Crisis and growing French nationalist sentiment prompted a charismatic Quebecer named René Lévesque to run for

During the 1970s, Canadian prime minister Pierre Trudeau (left) and Quebec premier René Lévesque (right) dominated the debate over Quebec's future.

office. Lévesque, who had founded the Parti Québécois in 1968, led his party to power in 1976. Although members of the PQ represented a wide ideological spectrum, they all shared a common dream—the creation of an independent Quebec. The PQ promised Quebecers a prosperous, self-governing territory that underscored Francophone ethnic pride and economic aspirations. The party quickly gained a strong following, and Lévesque was elected Quebec's premier later that year. Under Lévesque's leadership, the economy improved, providing more jobs for Quebecers. At the same time, support for sovereignty grew steadily.

In 1977 Quebec's National Assembly passed more laws to promote the French language. Bill 101 banned the use of any language other than French on public signs and limited access to English-language schools. According to the bill's provisions, children were allowed to attend Quebec's English-language schools only if one of their parents had received an English-language education in Quebec. Bill 101 also made French the only official language of Quebec's National Assembly and required firms with more than 100 employees to conduct their business affairs in French. Special agreements and exemptions allowed some companies to continue doing business in English.

After the bill passed, it was clear that the sovereigntists maintained a tight grip on Quebec's government. English-speaking Quebecers left the province in droves. Some emigrated to other parts of Canada, while many went to the United States. Political moderates and business leaders expressed concern that the flight of talented young Anglophones would hurt Quebec's economy.

In 1980 the PQ organized a referendum on what the party called sovereignty-association. Under the proposed sovereignty-association arrangement, Quebec would be independent but would still maintain strong ties with Canada. To avoid alienating potential sovereigntist supporters, however, organizers of the referendum left the terms intentionally vague. Some thought that sover-eignty-association meant that Quebec would continue to have strong economic ties with Canada, using Canadian currency and passports, while holding separate, independent control of Quebec's domestic and foreign affairs. But no definitive structure was outlined, and no consensus existed on how successful a sovereignty-association arrangement would be. When the idea was finally put to a vote in the 1980 referendum, only 40 percent of Quebecers voted yes. Opponents of the measure were able to raise sufficient voter concern about the referendum's vague meaning and its implications to make Quebecers vote against it.

Facing page: *A large and diverse country, Canada has always had difficulty maintaining a sense of national unity. Canada's 10 provinces and 3 federally run territories have had disputes over official languages, natural resources, and fishing rights.*

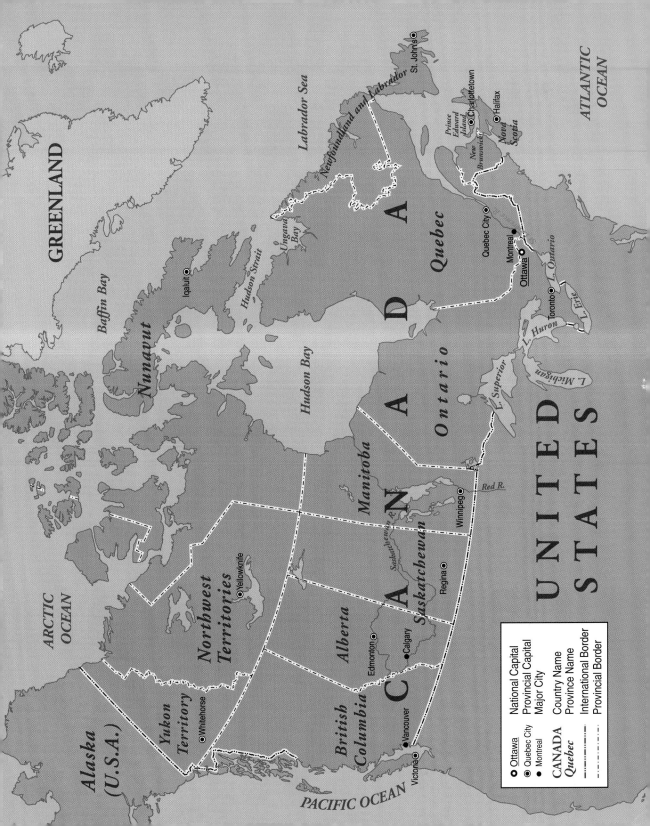

WAKE-UP CALL

The failure of the 1980 referendum considerably weakened the PQ and the sovereigntist cause. Its leaders became more moderate and dropped their strong push for independence. At the same time, public support for an independent Quebec declined to a meager 15 percent. Some observers speculated that the sovereigntist cause might fall apart entirely.

During the early 1980s, Prime Minister Trudeau continued his efforts to broker negotiations for resolution to the conflict with Quebec. In 1982 Canada modified the original terms of the British North America Act of 1867. In addition to including a Charter of Rights and Freedoms, the new act provided a mechanism for amending the Canadian constitution. Under the British North America Act, the British Parliament controlled Canada's constitution. For the first time, Canada was completely independent of Britain. All of Canada's provinces approved the document—with the exception of Quebec. This new basis for the Canadian federation became known as the Constitution Act of 1982.

While Quebec certainly wanted its independence from Britain, its leaders were upset that the constitution failed to protect Quebec's unique status as a French-speaking province within English Canada. Anticipating Quebec's objection to the new constitution, Trudeau called all of Canada's provincial leaders together—except Lévesque— for a secret midnight session to approve the deal. Quebec refused to sign Canada's constitution.

IN SEARCH OF COMPROMISE

In 1984 Brian Mulroney, another native Quebecer, succeeded Trudeau as prime minister. Mulroney shared Trudeau's mission of shaping a constitutional compromise that would bring Quebec into the Canadian fold. In 1987 Mulroney organized a meeting of Canada's 10 provincial leaders. At Meech Lake, a resort town in Quebec, the assembled leaders agreed to recognize Quebec

CP Picture Archive/Charles Mitchell

> "The attitude in English Canada is that if Meech Lake fails, it is not a catastrophe, but remember, the demands that Quebec is making now are the weakest demands it has ever made. . . . The nationalist movement [in Quebec] transcends party politics, and I predict that it will get even stronger if we don't have Meech Lake."
>
> Jules-Pascal Venne

as a distinct society and to grant Quebec veto power over any changes to the Canadian constitution that would affect the province. For the Meech Lake Accord to become binding, however, Canada's 10 provinces had to unanimously accept it within three years.

At first Canadians hoped that the Meech Lake Accord would be the long-awaited compromise. For the most part, French speakers in Quebec supported it—including Quebec premier Robert Bourassa, a member of the Liberal Party who had spearheaded the accord. In a panel debate before Canadians voted on the agreement, Jules-Pascal Venne, a Montreal lawyer and adviser to PQ leaders on constitutional issues, warned that if the accord was not ratified, the sovereigntist movement would gain momentum, not fall apart.

As Canada debated the future of the Meech Lake Accord, the PQ regained some of the popularity it had lost after the defeat of the 1980 referendum. By tapping into Québécois pride and economic problems in Quebec, the party's more radical sovereigntists asserted control over the revitalized party. After Lévesque's death in 1987, Jacques Parizeau became the PQ leader and vowed to continue the struggle for independence. After the shift in party leadership, the PQ debated internally on its future direction. PQ members decided to push for Quebec's complete independence from Canada.

Meanwhile, the Supreme Court of Canada ruled that Bill 101 (which banned the use of non-French words on commercial signs) violated Quebec's own charter of rights. French nationalist organizations in Quebec were outraged. In April 1988, they staged a massive public demonstration in support of defending the French language. Many observers were surprised by the sheer size of the gathering in Montreal and believed the rally helped breathe new life into the sovereigntist movement.

Later that year, Quebec lawmakers responded to the Supreme Court ruling by approving Bill 178, a law that prohibits restaurants, stores, and all other establishments that use outdoor advertising

Facing Page: Brian Mulroney (front) *and Canada's 10 provincial leaders announce the signing of the Meech Lake Accord, a set of constitutional reforms that attempted to satisfy Quebec's demands for constitutional change.*

A poster on the back of a truck expresses Anglophone sentiment about Bill 101.

BILL 101 – FASCIST

EVERYONE – FIGHT BACK NOW!

YOU HAVE LOST YOUR...

- CHILDREN
- ENGLISH SIGNS
- EMPLOYMENT
- ENGLISH INSTITUTIONS
- DIGNITY
- ENGLISH HERITAGE
- POLITICAL REPRESENTATION

ARE THESE NEXT TO GO?

- ENGLISH BOOKS
- ENGLISH FILMS, T.V., MUSIC
- ENGLISH NEWSPAPERS
- INTER-RACIAL ASSOCIATION
- ENGLISH EDUCATION
- ENGLISH IMMIGRATION
- THE FREEDOM TO ASSOCIATE

FREEDOM
SPEAKS OUT

FREEDOM NOW !

The Gazette, Montreal

from posting outdoor signs in English. Although the bill allowed English on indoor signs, it declared illegal the use of any non-French words on outdoor commercial signs. The provincial government established the Commission for the Protection of the French Language to help enforce the law. The government hired roving inspectors, whom Anglophones dubbed the "language police," to report violations. Violators could be subject to fines. Anglophones in Quebec and in the rest of the country strongly objected to Bill 178. They argued that the sign laws hindered their right to free speech as guaranteed by Canada's Charter of Rights and Freedoms.

Meanwhile, many English-speaking Canadians opposed a clause in the Meech Lake agreement that recognized Quebec as a distinct society. In other parts of Canada, leaders of the Reform Party argued that the accord was unfair. While it granted Quebec a special status, they said, it did not properly distribute power between Canada's federal government and its western provinces. In addition, many native peoples were concerned about the agreement and what it might mean for their future. They were also upset that governments were willing to try to meet Quebec's demands but had made little effort to address their issues of concern.

Ultimately, the Meech Lake Accord was scuttled when Manitoba and Newfoundland failed to ratify it. In Manitoba, Cree Indian legislator Elijah Harper played a key role in blocking the agreement. The defeat was a major setback to those struggling to maintain a united Canada.

In 1990, after the Meech Lake Accord fizzled, a group of conservative federalists and liberals from Quebec left their parties to form the independent Bloc Québécois. The founding of the BQ, a national equivalent to the PQ, marked the first time that the sovereigntist movement had achieved a presence in Canadian national politics. BQ support grew rapidly and it became the most popular national party in Quebec by the end of 1990. Lucien Bouchard, one of the PQ's most prominent ex-members, emerged as one of the BQ's best-known and most popular leaders.

ANOTHER ACCORD

Yet the federalists were not ready to give up. In 1992 Mulroney and other leaders worked out another constitutional reform package that came to be called the Charlottetown Accord. The agreement sought to win over groups that had opposed the Meech Lake Accord by promising greater political clout to thinly populated regions and a measure of self-government to native peoples. For Francophones the key clause stated, "Quebec constitutes within Canada a distinct society, which includes a French-speaking majority, a unique culture, and a civil law tradition." The clause also affirmed the right of Quebec's provincial government to preserve and promote the province's distinctiveness. A referendum on the accord was scheduled for October 26, 1992.

The Charlottetown Accord was controversial both in Quebec and throughout Canada, but for very different reasons. Parizeau and Bouchard attacked the agreement for not going far enough to enshrine Quebec's autonomy. Federalists in the provinces of western Canada opposed the Charlottetown Accord because they thought it gave too much to Quebec.

What about Us?

Zebedee Nungak, an Inuit leader who has represented his people for 20 years, provided his thoughts on Quebec sovereignty to a Fraser Institute Round Table audience on June 13, 1996. He told the audience that he's often frustrated when sovereigntist leaders refer to Quebec as a homogenous, distinct society, a homeland of French language and culture. In reality the northern two-thirds of Quebec is Inuit territory, not English or French. Nungak explained, "This is our home and native land, and we do not believe that we should be bandied about from jurisdiction to jurisdiction as we have been in the past, with absolutely no regard for how we feel, where we want to be, how we want to define our own relationship to the government."

The Quebec Inuit population has made it clear that it does not want to be part of an independent Quebec. Nungak outlined three alternatives: joining Nunavut, establishing a Nunavik territory and negotiating to become part of Canada, or forming some sort of union with the Cree Indians and becoming a part of Canada.

Native groups were split on the accord. Some thought that the agreement satisfied their needs. Others opposed the agreement because they felt that they deserved an even better deal. In the end, Canadians defeated the accord when only 4 out of Canada's 10 provinces voted in favor of it. Quebec rejected the accord.

Meanwhile, the war over language had quieted down somewhat. In 1993, due to Anglophone protest and to a ruling by the United Nations Committee on Human Rights, Bill 178 was amended. The committee cited the International Covenant on Civil and Political Rights when it ruled that Quebec could not prohibit languages other than French.

The new law, Bill 86, allowed English to be used on outdoor commercial signs as long as the same words also appeared in French and in more prominent type. The Commission for the Protection of the French Language was abolished in 1993. But some private citizens took charge of reporting violators themselves, snapping pictures to document the illegal use of English.

Certainly, the defeat of both the Charlottetown and the Meech Lake accords had convinced many Québécois that constitutional negotiations with English Canada were pointless. So hard-line sovereigntist Jacques Parizeau found an enthusiastic audience when he promised to hold another

referendum on independence if voters elected him as Quebec's next premier. Voters, frustrated by failed attempts to reach common ground with Anglophones, elected Parizeau in 1994.

In October 1995, Parizeau fulfilled his promise, sending Quebecers to the polls for a second time to decide whether or not Quebec should become independent.

OTHER GROUPS SPEAK OUT

As Quebecers debated their future status, specific ethnic groups in Quebec declared their intent to question the authority of an independent Quebec. Anglophones said they'd demand the right to remain Canadian citizens if Quebec separated. An official government poll found that 50 percent of Anglophones planned to leave the province if separation became a reality.

Some native leaders also clearly opposed Quebec independence, mistrusting the new authority's willingness to preserve and protect tribal lands. Days before the 1995 vote, the Cree and the Inuit held their own referendums on Quebec independence. They strongly supported

"[Sovereignty] is a necessity for Quebec . . . because we are a people, because we have always felt and behaved as such, because we live in a land where our ancestors settled almost [400] years ago, because we have a culture all of our own and have as our official language French, that sacred heritage preserved by the struggles, the fidelity and the courage of [12] generations."

Lucien Bouchard

In the weeks leading up to the referendum, Prime Minister Jean Chrétien (left) *and BQ leader Lucien Bouchard* (below) *vigorously promoted their views on the referendum. While Chrétien appealed to Canadian unity, Bouchard urged voters to acknowledge Quebec's unique identity.*

remaining part of Canada and called on the federal government to send troops to protect native lands in the event that Quebec separated from Canada. When all the votes were tallied, Quebecers defeated the second referendum on sovereignty, but it lost by the slimmest of margins—50.6 percent to 49.4 percent.

CONFLICT CONTINUES
In the late 1990s, the tension in Quebec remained very much alive. Some Francophones felt that they had to fight to keep their hard-won rights. In August 1996, Gilles Rhéaume, a crusader for French-language rights, picketed the Montreal Jewish Hospital after a reporter for the French language Radio-Canada Network alleged that he had been told to speak English during a hospital stay. Some hard-liners in the PQ have pushed to strengthen language laws by repealing Bill 86 and returning to French-only signs. They also supported the decision to bring back the Commission for the Protection of the French Language and the language inspectors who enforced Bill 178. And the PQ hasn't given up on holding another referendum on independence.

After the 1995 referendum, angry Anglophones claimed that Bouchard had tried to rig the voting. Since the referendum, Anglophones have been more vocal in their demand for equal linguistic and cultural rights.

Anglophones continue to fight for their right to speak freely and to communicate in English. Howard Galganov, a Montreal advertising executive and leading English-rights advocate holds views that are controversial even within the Anglophone community. Galganov organized a boycott of Montreal stores to protest any further restrictions of English on commercial signs. As president of the Quebec Political Action Committee (QPAC), Galganov targeted large retailers such as Radio Shack, Blockbuster Video, and others. According to Galganov, every merchant approached by QPAC agreed to post bilingual signs in their Quebec stores.

Federalist groups seek court rulings to prevent future referendums on sovereignty. In September 1996, Guy Bertrand, a Quebec City attorney and leading supporter of Canadian unity, attacked sovereigntist leaders for refusing to renounce their quest for independence. "By turning its back on democracy, refusing to respect the rule of law, the constitution and the courts, the Quebec government has taken an extremely dangerous step, placing the secessionist agenda above the law at the risk of plunging Quebec into chaos, anarchy, disorder, and endless confrontation," Bertrand said.

The ongoing conflict still affects the daily lives of people in Quebec, especially of those living in the Montreal area. It's possible that uncertainty about Quebec's future has made many foreign companies hesitant to invest in the province. Whatever the cause, 20 percent of Montreal's office and retail space is vacant. In the past two decades, many English-led companies and more than 150,000 Anglophone residents have left Quebec. More continue to emigrate each year. Many of those who leave are young and well educated, and their departure represents a severe economic loss to the

Young Anglophones Leaving Quebec

David Mulligan, a young engineer who graduated at the top of his class from McGill University in Montreal, is typical of Anglophones who have fled Quebec. In a 1996 letter to the *Montréal Gazette,* Mulligan explained why he was leaving the province. "In a normal democracy, the [1995 referendum] would have decided the question [of Quebec independence]," Mulligan wrote. "In Quebec... the government keeps holding referendums at public expense until it gets the answer that it wants. This point is of deep concern to me, because it puts any job that I would hold in Quebec at constant risk. I cannot continue to put my family in situations where they do not know whether the next paycheque [sic] is coming.... I now believe that there is no future for my family in Quebec. There is a vicious cycle of continuing instability that leads to reduced foreign confidence, more people leaving to find jobs, a reduced tax base, a growing deficit, reduced services and higher taxes for those left behind."

province. Quebec's higher-than-average unemployment rate hasn't helped matters. According to a November 1997 *National Geographic* article, one in five Montrealers was out of work that month. At the same time, 22 percent of those residing in Montreal lived below the poverty line. Food banks have become the fastest-growing businesses in Montreal, feeding about 150,000 Quebecers annually.

In 1998 the Canadian Supreme Court agreed to decide the question of whether or not Quebec could legally secede from the rest of Canada. In August of that year, the court's nine justices, three of them from Quebec, ruled that Quebec could not unilaterally declare independence from Canada. On the other hand, the justices declared that if the sovereigntists won a decisive referendum victory, Canada would be required to negotiate the country's possible breakup. The wording of any future referendum, however, would have to clearly and unequivocally ask Quebecers to vote Oui or Non on the independence question. Both sovereigntists and federalists claimed that the Supreme Court's decision was a victory for their side.

ELECTION ANSWERS QUESTIONS

On November 30, 1998, Quebecers went to the polls to elect their next premier. Although it was a tight race, the PQ incumbent, Lucien Bouchard, won 44.3 percent of the vote. He edged out the Quebec Liberal Party candidate, Jean Charest, who garnered 42.8 percent of the vote. The results echoed the outcome of the 1994 elections. However, the popular vote went to the Liberal Party, indicating that Quebecers voted to elect a government, not to determine the future of their province. According to campaign polls, 70 percent of Quebecers didn't want another referendum on sovereignty. In his victory speech, Bouchard seemed to take his cue from voters when he didn't mention holding a referendum on sovereignty anytime soon. Only time will tell if backlash from PQ hard-liners will force Bouchard to change his mind. ⊕

CHAPTER

4

WHAT'S BEING DONE TO SOLVE THE PROBLEM

As Quebecers and the rest of Canada search for ways to resolve the conflict, it's important to keep in mind that both options—sovereignty and renewed federalism—are legitimate, democratic forms of government. One is not better nor worse than the other, and each system has its positive and negative aspects.

Regardless of the outcome, leaders on both sides of the issue will have to agree upon a clear division of power between the federal and provincial governments. Reaching such a consensus will not be easy, as it requires leaders to adjust the very structure of Canadian federalism—a system that has swung back and forth between centralization and decentralization of power throughout the country's history.

Because conflict resolution relies heavily on the restructuring of the federal and provincial governments, most efforts to reach a consensus have been legislative. As in any dispute, each side has brought its own requirements and ideas to the negotiating table.

THE FEDERALIST POSITION

Federalists favor a united Canada that includes Quebec as a fully functioning member of the Canadian federation. Before the 1995 referendum, the Liberal Party was the leading federalist party in Quebec, and party leader Daniel Johnson headed the anti-independence campaign. While Johnson and other liberal leaders supported a united Canada, they also expressed a willingness to back

legislation that would officially recognize Quebec's distinct status by granting the province unique rights and privileges within the Canadian federation. In the final week of the referendum campaign, for example, Jean Chrétien, then Canada's prime minister, promised Quebec's leaders that he would support the province's right to veto constitutional amendments that would affect the province.

Some Quebec federalists criticized Johnson and the Liberal Party for not taking a stronger stand against Québécois nationalism. The anti-sovereigntist Equality Party criticized the liberals for joining the PQ in its quest to give Quebec status as a distinct society.

During the referendum campaign, federalists warned

that an independent Quebec would face severe economic hardship and would be isolated economically, politically, and culturally from the rest of North America. A few days before the referendum, Chrétien, a Quebecer himself, addressed Canadians in a nationally televised speech. "It is not only the future of Quebec that will be decided on Monday [October 30, 1995]. It is the future of all Canada. The decision that will be made is serious and irreversible. With deep, deep consequences."

Federalists argue that French culture is already thriving in a united Canada and that there are too many troubling uncertainties surrounding separation to make it worthwhile. Some Canadian constitutional scholars, for example, assert that an independent Quebec should not get to keep two-thirds of its territory, because the land in question was given to the province by the Canadian Parliament and has no connection with historic French Canada.

FEDERAL GOVERNMENT EFFORTS

Based on these beliefs, the federal government has

In 1995 Daniel Johnson, head of the Liberal Party, celebrated the Non victory. In recent years, the Liberal Party has backed efforts to acknowledge Quebec's distinct character in the constitution.

worked hard to foster unity. Stephen Dion, a federalist from Montreal and Canada's minister of intergovernmental affairs, leads many efforts. Prime Minister Chrétien gave Dion a mandate to explore constitutional change within the provinces. After his study, Dion proposed that, for Canada to remain intact, the country must take three steps toward reconciliation. First, lawmakers must reform the constitution to better divide power and responsibility between Canada's federal and provincial governments. Second, Canada must recognize

Quebec as a distinct society. And third, all Canadians must take part in a celebration of the nation's strengths.

In February 1996, Parliament approved legislation giving Quebec and three other provincial "blocs" veto power over changes to Canada's constitution. In September 1997, nine of the ten provincial premiers—minus Quebec's—met in Calgary to attempt to forge constitutional compromises that would accommodate Quebec's requests. Quebec premier Lucien Bouchard refused to attend. Bouchard and other ardent

CP Picture Archive/Tom Hanson

Mr. Dion Goes to Ottawa

As Canada's minister of intergovernmental affairs, Stephen Dion *(left)* is an advocate for national reconciliation. He has worked to persuade Canada's provinces to recognize Quebec as a "distinct society." In numerous speeches and public appearances throughout Canada, Dion stresses, "It is time, more than ever, to explain why Canada is a great value, and why Quebecers, who have contributed so much to this model of tolerance, openness, and quality, must stay in Canada."

In many ways, however, Dion is an unlikely choice to lead the unity crusade. The 41-year-old teacher had virtually no political experience when Canada's prime minister selected him for the post in November 1995. Dion is a distinguished scholar with a doctorate in political sociology from the Institut de Politics in Paris. His students at the Université de Montréal knew him as an objective lecturer who kept his personal opinions out of the classroom. He is more comfortable carrying his speeches in a worn knapsack than in a black leather attaché case. He didn't seek his current job and doesn't necessarily want to keep it.

On the issue of Canadian unity, however, Dion speaks with missionary zeal. "Too many of the people who believe in Canada are either passive or in despair towards the future of our country," he says. "Passivity and despair—we must free ourselves from these attitudes if we are to save Canada."

To remain a strong and united country, Dion argues, Canada must be willing to reach a compromise with Quebec. He also favors reforms to the Canadian constitution that would grant more power and autonomy to all the provincial governments.

This very single-minded devotion has prompted critics to charge that he is politically naive and that his stubbornness and brusque manner are needlessly offensive—even to fellow Liberal Party members. Provincial leaders in Manitoba, Alberta, and British Columbia complain that Dion doesn't appreciate the depth of opposition to granting Quebec special status in the Canadian federation. On the other side, a member of the Bloc Québécois once chidingly called him "the apostle of infinite love."

Despite the criticism, and despite the continued strength of Quebec's sovereigntist movement, Dion remains optimistic about Canada's future—if the country's people work together. "The voices of despair have been saying that the secession of Quebec is inevitable, that there is nothing we can do as governments or citizens to prevent it," he says. "To combat this despair, this resignation, I want to say that we must have hope, and that we have good reason to look to the future of Canada with hope."

sovereigntists felt that any agreement reached at Calgary would provide merely symbolic rather than substantive measures to ensure Quebec's distinctiveness within Canada. Nevertheless, all nine attendees agreed to a plan that came to be called the Calgary Declaration.

The Calgary Declaration proposed a seven-pronged approach to establishing Canadian unity, including validations of diversity, tolerance, citizen equality, and the mutual respect of the provincial and federal governments. The more controversial points include declarations that all provinces have "equality of status," that Quebec's society has a "unique character" (rather than "distinct," as Quebec has long insisted), and that "if any future constitutional change confers power on one province, these must be available to all provinces." Sovereigntists regarded the recognition of Quebec's "uniqueness" as a symbolic gesture and continued to push Canada's leaders to regard Quebec as a "distinct society." This designation, they argued, would allow the province to have more power to regulate its inter-nal affairs than is granted to Canada's nine other provinces.

The response to the Calgary Declaration has been mixed. Although the declaration was eventually approved by all of Canada's Anglophone parliaments (except Nova Scotia's), federalist leaders, including Chrétien, feared that it didn't go far enough to satisfy Quebec's Francophone leaders. They were right. Quebec's sovereigntist leaders quickly dismissed the declaration as mere wordplay and bad faith.

The Canadian federal government had made attempts to recognize and to accommodate Quebec's unique status within Canada. In December 1995, for example, Parliament passed a resolution recognizing Quebec's distinct language, culture, and civil law. Chrétien strengthened Quebec's representation in his cabinet by appointing Stephen Dion to serve as Canada's minister of national unity. While Quebec's sovereigntist leaders generally regard these measures as a step in the right direction, they also argue that the efforts did not go far enough to recognize and safeguard the province's language, history, and culture.

THE SOVEREIGNTIST POSITION

Sovereigntist leaders tell Quebecers why they want Quebec to become an independent country. They discuss economic issues such as Quebec's unusually high unemployment rate, but for the most part, sovereigntists appeal to Québécois' strong sense of civic pride. The sovereigntists emphasize the unique status of Quebec and its French-speaking majority. They argue that Quebecers cannot achieve their true destiny as a people by remaining in a country where they are the minority. They highlight that all past attempts at constitutional reform, which would have given Quebec broader powers within the Canadian federation, have failed. If the Québécois don't choose the path of independence, the sovereigntists have warned, they will eventually be swallowed up by English Canada.

In seeking sovereignty, Quebecers have stated that they do not think that they are better than Canadians from other provinces—just different. With such differences in

Every year Francophones in Montreal celebrate their history and culture during the St. Jean Baptiste Parade. Such expressions of Francophone pride assure that the sovereignty issue will be around for years to come.

language, culture, and social and economic vision, sovereigntists believe that Quebec would be better off on its own. They've proposed a set of guidelines to help ease the transition to sovereignty and to foster relations between Quebec and Canada after the split.

At the same time, sovereigntist leaders have tried to ease concerns about independence. Quebec's desire to control its own economy and to promote its culture does not mean that the province would want to sever economic ties with Canada. Quebec recognizes the benefits of trade with Canada and proposes an economic partnership. Under such an agreement, Quebec hopes to maintain economic ties, promote free trade, and share a common currency with Canada. Quebec would also seek inclusion in the North American Free Trade Agreement (NAFTA). The new country, moreover, would meet

all of its financial obligations to Canada, including paying its share of the national debt.

Sovereigntist leaders also try to reassure minority groups that they would be treated well in the new Quebec. More specifically, sovereigntists promise that, in an independent Quebec, native groups would continue to have the same degree of self-rule and autonomy that they currently enjoy. An independent Quebec would respect the rights of Anglophones and Allophones, allowing them to continue to control their own English-language schools, colleges, and universities. Sovereigntists assure these groups that they would be able to access vital government services, health and social services, and public broadcasting channels in English. Quebec also plans to request that Anglophones living in the province be allowed to keep their Canadian citizenship.

THE SOVEREIGNTIST PLAN
Throughout the life of the sovereigntist movement, leaders have provided clear lists of their requirements to the federal government. After the nine other Canadian provinces signed the constitution in

1982, sovereigntist hopes of ever reaching a compromise with the rest of Canada were almost dashed. Yet the movement tried again, drawing up a list of five conditions that would have to be addressed before Quebec would recognize the constitution.

Quebec premier and Liberal Party leader Robert Bourassa presented these conditions to Canada in 1985. First, Quebec would be recognized by the rest of the provinces as a distinct society. Second, Quebec would have the power to veto any proposed changes to the constitution. Third, Quebec asked for a guarantee from the other provinces that a fair number of judges from Quebec would be appointed to Canada's Supreme Court. Fourth, the province proposed that all Canadian provinces have the freedom to reject participation in federal government programs with full financial compensation. And lastly, Quebec requested more control over immigration policies within its borders.

The federal government responded to Quebec's requirements by including them in the Meech Lake Accord in 1987. When the accord fell

Bouchard Reaches Out

In March 1996, Quebec premier Lucien Bouchard spoke at the Centaur Theater in Montreal. Bouchard's audience was a group of prominent Anglophones who were eager to hear what the PQ government planned to do after recent defeat in the referendum on sovereignty. It was a historic gesture—the first time that a Francophone prime minister of Quebec had so publicly reached out to such a broad segment of the Anglophone community. Many hoped Bouchard and the PQ would seek to mend fences with the federalists.

"I know that the road from words to acts, from intentions to achievement, has to start somewhere," Bouchard told the packed house. "I know full well that to have a dialogue, more than one person has to speak. But someone has to make the first move. That's why I'm here." While Bouchard acknowledged the many issues that still divide Anglophones and Francophones—including control over education, access to government and health services, and Quebec's future relationship with Canada—he focused on shared values such as democracy, equality, freedom of expression, and diversity. Ultimately, however, Bouchard appealed to a shared sense of pride in their identity as Quebecers. "It's good to know there is one unalterable truth we can cling to: the knowledge that in the end we are all Quebecers, *nous sommes tous Québécois,* we all love Quebec—because Quebec is home."

Reaction to Bouchard's speech in the Anglophone community was cautious, yet upbeat. Many of those in the audience said the conciliatory tone of his remarks helped to heal the bitter words of Jacques Parizeau, Bouchard's predecessor, after the PQ lost the 1995 referendum. In his post-referendum speech, Parizeau had blamed the sovereigntists' defeat on "money and the ethnic vote." His reference to the ethnic vote particularly angered Quebec's Allophone community (including Greeks, Italians, and Jews), which makes up about 10 percent of the province's population. These comments also upset many non-Francophones who had long suspected that there were racist undertones to the sovereigntist movement.

apart over debates about the distinct society clause, sovereigntist leaders decided that independence was the only means to achieve their goal of building a more prosperous Quebec.

The federal government tried to further negotiations with the Charlottetown Accord. But Quebec's leaders thought the agreement watered down the distinct status provision even more than the Meech Lake Accord did. Resolved that coming to any kind of agreement with the federal government was unlikely, Quebec sovereigntists began working to build up support within the province for a Oui vote for sovereignty.

The federal government's most recent efforts to bridge the gap—the drafting of the Calgary Declaration—seemed insulting to sovereigntists. The declaration replaced the "distinct society" status that Quebecers had requested with what the federal government dubbed "unique character"—a standing that bestowed no new powers on Quebec that weren't also granted to other provinces. To Quebecers, even those in favor of federalism, the declaration fell far short of meeting Quebec's demands. Sovereigntists formulated a plan.

Quebec is not about to declare sovereignty against the wishes of its citizens. Referenda remain the best way to gauge public opinion on sovereignty for Quebec. Sovereigntists have established three rules to guide Quebec's quest for independence. First and foremost, Quebecers have the right to decide the future of their province. In fact, the Canadian constitution makes no reference to provinces seeking sovereignty—more specifically, it does not forbid it. So it is not against federal law to declare sovereignty, should the people of a province vote in favor of it. Second, Quebec must abide by the internationally held rules of democracy. And third, Quebec must retain its territorial boundaries.

In the event that a majority of Quebecers does vote in favor of sovereignty, political leaders in Quebec would initiate talks with the federal government to establish an economic and monetary partnership with Canada. An independent Quebec would promise to pay off its debts to Canada, as well as its debts to international lenders on the province's behalf. Quebec would gain

Providing a Forum

The Fraser Institute, a leading economic think tank based in Vancouver, British Columbia, plays an important role in shaping and expanding the nation's public policy debates. Quebec's request for sovereignty has been a topic of discussion at the institute for many years as the group works to come up with possible solutions to the issue.

Through roundtable discussions and monthly forums, the Fraser Institute has hosted speakers from all sides of the conflict. Daniel Turp, president of the Bloc Québécois Policy Committee, addressed the institute on March 27, 1996. Three months later, on June 13, 1996, Zebedee Nungak spoke to a Fraser Institute audience. At the end of each roundtable discussion, audience members are invited to ask questions of the guest speaker. The hope is that a workable solution will come to light from listening to all sides of the story.

the power to pass laws and levy taxes within the province and to participate directly in its international affairs. After so many failed attempts to mend fences with Canada, sovereigntists believe that the establishment of an autonomous Quebec is the best option.

BUILDING BRIDGES

Amid the flurry of legislative negotiations between the two sides, ordinary people have found ways to make their voices heard. Aside from groups promoting the cause of one side or the other—such as the Council for Canadian Unity, Citoyens Ensemble (Citizens Together), Intellectuals for Sovereignty, and Jeunes Souverainistes (Young Sovereigntists)—there are many organizations searching for common ground between the two sides. In Quebec itself, a number of informal and private political, religious, and civic groups are working to build bridges between sovereigntists and federalists. Forum Action Québec and Citoyens de la Nation (Citizens for a Democratic Nation-CDN)—are two such groups.

Many Francophones and Anglophones hope that the province of Quebec can find a way to maintain its identity and remain a part of Canada.

Forum Action Québec, a nonprofit, nonpartisan group of young Anglophone college and graduate students, is dedicated to fostering dialogue between Quebec's French- and English-speaking communities. Forum Action Québec has criticized leaders on both sides of the conflict for using inflated or divisive rhetoric in discussions of Quebec sovereignty. On March 14, 1996, Forum Action Québec sponsored a conference titled "Facing the Future: Building Quebec Together." Francophone and Anglophone speakers at the conference focused on social and economic concerns shared by people in both linguistic groups.

CDN, a nonpolitical movement led by former sovereigntist Guy Bertrand, is dedicated to forming a network of Canadian citizens committed to creating a responsible society within the democratic realm. CDN also works to protect the rights and freedoms of all Quebecers. Among the group's specific goals are the opening up of permanent communication between citizens and the improvement of the political, economic, and social stability throughout Canada.

While past efforts to resolve the sovereignty issue have not produced an acceptable compromise, these and other groups are actively working to keep alive hopes of a peaceful solution. Meanwhile, voters in Quebec voiced their weariness in the 1998 elections when they voted against holding another referendum. For the time being, Quebecers appear willing to work within a united Canada toward a better Quebec. ⊕

EPILOGUE*

Although the results of the November 30, 1998, elections stopped Lucien Bouchard and PQ members from talking about sovereignty for a few months, the issue was back on the table by the spring of 1999. In early February, at the first big PQ meeting since the election, Bouchard spoke of sovereignty with renewed resolution, referring to Quebec's independence as, "a conviction and a necessity." At the same gathering, Bouchard announced that the next PQ convention would be postponed from the fall of 1999 to the spring of 2000, to give the party time to come up with a new strategy for achieving sovereignty.

In the meantime, Bouchard is busy representing Quebec abroad. During a March 1999 tour of Europe, Bouchard met with Jordi Pujol, president of the Spanish autonomous region of Catalonia, who encouraged Quebec to seek sovereignty. French president Jacques Chirac greeted Bouchard with a welcome usually reserved for heads of state. In April 1999, Bouchard was on the road again to meet with U.S. business leaders in New York. Such efforts to connect with foreign governments imply that the PQ's push for sovereignty will not die anytime soon.

*Please note: The information presented in *Quebec: Province Divided* was current at the time of the book's publication. For the most recent information about the conflict, look for articles in the international section of U.S. daily newspapers. *The Economist*, a weekly magazine, and *Maclean's*, a Canadian weekly newsmagazine, are also good sources for up-to-date information. You may wish to access, via the Internet, *The Montreal Gazette* at http://www.montrealgazette.com or, for front-page news stories from Canadian newspapers, access http://www.infomart.ca/todays_news/index.html.

CHRONOLOGY

1500s   Speakers of Algonquian languages—the Algonquin, Micmac, and Cree—inhabit what would become Quebec.

1534   Jacques Cartier arrives at what comes to be known as the Gaspé Peninsula and claims the area for France.

1608   Failing to find a new Asian trade route, French explorer Samuel de Champlain establishes the first permanent French settlement in North America.

1670   After gaining interest in New France's fur trade, Great Britain establishes its first permanent settlement at Hudson Bay.

1754–1763   The French and Indian War rages in North America while the Seven Years' War occurs in Europe.

1759   General James Wolfe attacks Quebec City. Britain assumes the rule of Quebec from France.

1763   The Seven Years' War ends. The Royal Proclamation of 1763 redraws Quebec's boundaries and replaces the French judicial system with English civil and criminal law.

1774   British Parliament passes the Québec Act.

1775   American general Benedict Arnold leads the Continental Army's invasion of Quebec.

1791   British Parliament passes the Constitutional Act of 1791, dividing Quebec into Upper and Lower Canada.

1837–1838   British soldiers defeat the Patriotes in battles near Montreal.

1839   In the Durham Report, Lord Durham recommends that the government's legislative branch control the executive branch.

1840   Britain passes the Act of Union, which merges Lower Canada and Upper Canada into a single colony. Article 41 makes English the only official language of Canada.

1847   French Canadian Louis-Hippolyte LaFontaine and English Canadian Robert Baldwin, leaders of the Reform Party, win national elections. The British appoint Lord Elgin as the new governor-general of Canada.

1848   Lord Elgin argues to repeal Article 41, restoring the language rights of French Canadians.

1867   Canada becomes a confederation under the British North America Act of 1867.

1885   Louis Riel, leader of the Métis, stages the North-West Rebellion.

1896   Liberal Party leader, Sir Wilfred Laurier, wins national elections to become the first French-Canadian prime minister of Canada.

1914   Britain enters World War I.

1928   Quebec's economy is threatened when winter-wheat crops fail.

1936   Union Nationale party candidate Maurice Duplessis is elected premier of Quebec.

1939   World War II begins. Voters reject the Union Nationale party in elections.

1944   Canadian prime minister drafts 16,000 soldiers into service. Duplessis is reelected.

1948   Duplessis makes the French fleur-de-lis the official symbol of Quebec.

1959   Maurice Duplessis dies.

1960   Liberal Party member Jean Lesage is elected premier of Quebec. The Quiet Revolution begins.

1962   Lesage and the Liberal Party win reelection with the slogan, "Masters in our own home."

1963   The Front de Libération du Québec claims responsibility for a wave of terrorist bombings.

1964   The British monarch visits Canada to mark a century of confederation. The FLQ robs a Canadian company, International Firearms, of $50,000 and kills the company's vice president.

1965   Canadian prime minister Lester Pearson establishes the first Royal Commission on Bilingualism and Biculturalism.

1968   Riots erupt over language rights in the Montreal suburb of St. Leonard. The FLQ detonates bombs at McGill University and at the Montreal Stock Exchange, injuring 27 people. Pierre Elliot Trudeau is elected Canada's new prime minister.

1969   Trudeau backs the Official Languages Act, making French and English the official languages of Canada.

1970   During the October Crisis, the FLQ kidnaps British trade commissioner James Cross and kills Quebec cabinet minister Pierre LaPorte. Trudeau invokes the War Measures Act.

1971   The FLQ breaks up.

1976   Parti Québécois founder, René Lévesque, is elected Quebec's premier.

1977   Quebec's National Assembly passes Bill 101, which bans the use of any language other than French on public signs and limits access to English-language schools.

1980   The Parti Québécois organizes the first referendum on sovereignty-association. Only 40 percent of Quebecers vote yes.

1982   The Constitution Act of 1982 states that Great Britain's monarch is head of state. Canada modifies the original terms of the British North America Act of 1867 to include a Charter of Rights and Freedoms and a means for amending the Canadian constitution.

1984   Brian Mulroney, a native Quebecer, succeeds Trudeau as prime minister.

1987   The Meech Lake Accord grants Quebec veto power over any changes to the Canadian constitution that affect the province. Lévesque dies and Jacques Parizeau assumes leadership of the PQ.

1988   French nationalist organizations stage a mass public demonstration to defend the French language. Lawmakers approve Bill 178, which prohibits restaurants, stores, and all who use outdoor advertising from posting signs in English. The Commission for the Protection of the French Language is established.

1990   Meech Lake Accord fizzles. Conservative federalists and Quebec liberals form the Bloc Québécois.

1992   Mulroney and other leaders hammer out the Charlottetown Accord, which promises greater political clout to sparsely populated regions.

1993   Bill 178 is amended to Bill 86, which allows the use of English on indoor signs as long as the same words appear in French in more prominent type. The Commission for the Protection of the French Language is abolished.

1994   Voters elect Jacques Parizeau as premier of Quebec.

1995   Second referendum on Quebec independence fails.

1996   PQ hard-liners attempt to revoke Bill 86. Guy Bertrand, a Quebec City attorney and supporter of Canadian unity, attacks sovereigntist leaders for refusing to give up their quest for independence.

1998   Nine justices of the Canadian Supreme Court rule that Quebec cannot unilaterally declare independence from Canada. Lucien Bouchard is elected premier of Quebec. Quebecers vote against holding another referendum on sovereignty.

SELECTED BIBLIOGRAPHY

Bothwell, Robert, et al. *Canada since 1945: Power, Politics, and Provincialism.* Toronto: University of Toronto Press, 1989.

Carens, Joseph H. *Is Quebec Nationalism Just? Perspectives from Anglophone Canada.* Montreal: McGill-Queen's University Press, 1995.

Lemco, Jonathan. *Turmoil in the Peaceable Kingdom: The Quebec Sovereignty Movement and Its Implications for Canada and the United States.* Toronto: University of Toronto Press, 1994.

Pinard, M. "The Dramatic Reemergence of the Quebec Independence Movement." *Journal of International Affairs.* January 1, 1992.

Richler, Mordecai. *Oh Canada! Oh Quebec! Requiem for a Divided Country.* New York: Alfred A. Knopf, 1992.

Schnurmacher, Thomas. *Canada Is Not a Real Country.* Toronto: ECW Press, 1996.

Turner, Craig. "Creating a New Nation from French Quebec." *Los Angeles Times.* December 11, 1994.

INDEX

ABOUT THE AUTHOR

Peter Kizilos is an award-winning author and communications consultant who lives in Minneapolis, Minnesota. He has written articles for major state and national publications and several books, including *South Africa: Nation in Transition, Tibet: Disputed Land* and, with Jackie Nink Pflug, *Miles to Go Before I Sleep: My Grateful Journey Back from the Hijacking of Egyptair Flight 648*. For his commitment to leadership in public affairs, Peter was named a Mondale Fellow by the University of Minnesota's Hubert H. Humphrey Institute of Public Affairs. Peter received his B.A., cum laude, from Yale University and an M.A. in area studies from the University of Michigan at Ann Arbor.

ABOUT THE CONSULTANTS

Andrew Bell-Fialkoff, *World in Conflict* series consultant, is a specialist on nationalism, ethnicity, and ethnic conflict. He is the author of *Ethnic Cleansing*, published by St. Martin's Press in 1996, and has written numerous articles for *Foreign Affairs* and other journals. He is writing a book on the role of migration in the history of the Eurasian Steppe. Bell-Fialkoff lives in Bradford, Massachusetts.

Pierre Coulombe is a Desjardins visiting professor at McGill University's Québec Studies Program. He holds a Ph.D. in political science from the University of Western Ontario. His research interests and publications include language policy, Québec nationalism, and Canadian federalism. He is a member of the Groupe de recherche sur les sociétés plurinationales.

SOURCES OF QUOTED MATERIAL

p. 26 Michael Jung, "Quebec Separatists Defeated by a Whisker," *The Independent*, 31 October 1995; pp. 26–27 "Montreal through a Lens Darkly," *Maclean's*, 14 October 1996, 11; p. 28 "Winds of Change," *Maclean's*, 4 March 1996, 26; p. 29 Tu Thanh Ha, "Reconciliation Eludes Two Solitudes," *The Globe & Mail*, 10 March 1997; p. 45 Quoted by Mrs. Francine Lalonde in House of Commons of Canada debates, 35th Parliament, 3 June 1996, on the House of Commons of Canada Website, http://www.parl.gc.ca/english /hansard//055_96-06-03/055GO2E.html#3341; p. 59 "In Search of National Unity: Five Experts Examine the Options," *Maclean's*, 20 March 1989, 28; p. 61 Quoted in the transcript of Zebedee Nungak's Speech to a Fraser Institute Roundtable audience, Vancouver, 13 June 1996, on the Fraser Institute's Website, http://www.fraserinstitute.ca; p. 62 Speech given at the opening of the National Convention of the Bloc Québécois, Palais de Congrès, Montreal, 7 April 1995; p. 64 (pull quote) Brenda Branswell, "A Man with a Mission: Quebec's Howard Galganov Fights for Anglophone Rights," *Maclean's*, 16 September 1996, 16; p. 64 (main text) Terrance Wills, "More Key Players," *Montreal Gazette*, 20 August 1998; p. 68 (top) E. Kaye Fulton, "Playing Hardball," *Maclean's*, 13 January 1996, 18; p. 68 (middle) "Canada's Communities and the Hope for Canadian Unity," an address by the President of the Privy Council and Minister of Intergovernmental Affairs, Stephen Dion, before the Federation of Canadian Municipalities, Calgary, 2 June 1996; p. 68 (bottom) E. Kaye Fulton, "Playing Hardball," *Maclean's*, 13 January 1996, 18; p. 71 (top and bottom) "Bouchard Extends Hand to Anglos: Excerpts from Premier Lucien Bouchard's Address to Anglophones March 11," *Montreal Gazette*, 12 March 1996.